Policing Matters

Police Ethics and Values

Policing Matters

Police Ethics and Values

Allyson MacVean and Peter Neyroud

Series editors

P A J Waddington

Martin Wright

Los Angeles | London | New Delhi
Singapore | Washington DC

www.learningmatters.co.uk

Los Angeles | London | New Delhi
Singapore | Washington DC

www.learningmatters.co.uk

Learning Matters
An imprint of SAGE Publications Ltd
1 Oliver's Yard
55 City Road
London EC1Y 1SP

SAGE Publications Inc.
2455 Teller Road
Thousand Oaks, California 91320

SAGE Publications India Pvt Ltd
B 1/I 1 Mohan Cooperative Industrial Area
Mathura Road
New Delhi 110 044

SAGE Publications Asia-Pacific Pte Ltd
3 Church Street
#10-04 Samsung Hub
Singapore 049483

Library of Congress Control Number: 2011945606

British Library Cataloguing in Publication Data

A catalogue record for this book is available from
the British Library

ISBN: 978 0 85725 385 9

Editor: Julia Morris
Development editor: Jennifer Clark
Production controller: Chris Marke
Project management: Diana Chambers
Marketing manager: Zoe Seaton
Copy-editor: Sue Edwards
Cover design: Toucan Designs
Typeset by: Kelly Winter
Printed by: MPG Books Group

Contents

v

1 Introduction to police ethics and values

Introduction

It is frequently the police who must take responsibility for the guarding of the boundaries where the actions of one individual have unacceptable consequences for others or for society at large.

(Jack Straw, 2001 in Neyroud and Beckley, 2001)

Ethics are a critical component of policing. Unlike other professions, such as medicine, law and accounting, the police do not have a code of ethics. Doctors undertake specialised training in medical ethics and are required, as part of the process of becoming a doctor, to accept the principles and philosophy of the Hippocratic Oath. This is because it is acknowledged within the profession of medicine that there are complex ethical decisions that doctors are required to make and that specific ethical training and support should be provided (Scottish Qualifications Authority (SQA), 2007). If it is accepted that policing is equally complex and demanding, with many ethical dilemmas, an understanding of ethics and ethical behaviour provides a framework and set of values that can guide an individual to make the right judgements and do the right things, for the right reasons – things that are morally correct.

There are two key aspects in relation to making the right judgements and doing the right things. The first is that police officers are primarily guided by the criminal law they are sworn to uphold. An ethical framework assists them in the application of discretion when preventing crime and enforcing the law. The second aspect is ethical judgement in administering the expenditure of public money upon which, arguably, government has placed greater emphasis since the 1980s than on upholding the integrity of the criminal law and the criminal justice system.

Pollock (1998) argues that the study of ethics is particularly important for criminal justice practitioners in general, and the police in particular, because:

- they are empowered with significant discretion to make decisions that affect the life, liberty and property of members of the community;

- they are empowered to use force in certain situations;

- they have a duty to enforce the law;

- they have a duty to protect the rights of members of the community;

- they are public servants and, therefore, as the appointed guardians of the public's interests, they must demonstrate high standards of integrity;

- they are authorised to use intrusive, covert and deceptive methods to detect and investigate crime;

- they have a crucial role in protecting hard-to-reach and vulnerable groups – thus they are the ultimate gatekeepers of citizenship and respectability.

(adapted from Pollock, 1998, pp3–4; Neyroud and Beckley, 2001, p38)

As we will demonstrate, the relationship between theories and principles of ethics and practical decision making in a policing environment is intricate and complex. Ethical decision making often requires *judgement* and not simply deductive reasoning. This involves making moral decisions about what is right or wrong, reasonable or unreasonable, deliberate or an accident. Thus, ethical decisions are equally about *doing the right things as much as doing things right.*

However, the challenge for policing is that the police are required to uphold and enforce the law regardless of the law's moral content. For example, the Criminal Procedure and Investigations Act 1996 makes it quite clear that the police role is to discover and present all relevant evidence, both inculpatory and exculpatory, and not to present just the evidence that a police officer has deemed relevant on the basis of what he or she may consider to be morally right or wrong. It is for this reason that ethical policing is so significant.

The day-to-day decisions made by police officers in undertaking their duties can make a difference to the outcomes of any situation. Consequently, police officers and police forces are now increasingly being asked to account not just for the decisions they make, but also for the way they have made them. Therefore, an understanding of ethics and an ability to relate theory to practice is now an essential part of a police officer's portfolio (Neyroud and Beckley, 2001). However, while the book provides details of the codes as set out by various police organisations, it must be remembered that ethical policing is not characterised by a distinctive type of ethics but is defined by the behaviour and culture of both the individual and organisation. Therefore, as we will learn, ethics are subjective.

Overview

This chapter will introduce key concepts of police ethics and values, including theories of ethics and their application in a practical policing context. These theories and concepts will be explored in greater depth using specific policing issues throughout the book.

Chapter 2 explores the characteristics of a profession and how these can be applied to the police organisation. It examines the principles for a code of ethics and considers how such a code may be beneficial to policing. It further highlights the current code of conduct for the police, and the merits and demerits of this in relation to acceptable and ethical behaviour.

Chapter 3 examines the issues of police culture in relation to ethical policing. It considers the role of culture and its influence on ethical and unethical police behaviour. In particular, it reviews how police discretion can facilitate or challenge deviant or corrupt police behaviour.

Chapter 4 examines not only how discrimination and prejudice can impact on policing ethnic minority groups, but also how it affects minority groups who work within the police service. In particular, it examines the Scarman Report, the Macpherson Inquiry and the Gender Agenda to understand how discrimination was conceptualised and understood within the broader context of policing. It explores how an understanding of your own values and prejudices may influence, either wittingly or unwittingly, your police practice.

Chapter 5 explores the nature of leadership and, in particular, leadership in policing. We have discussed the relationship between leadership and ethical behaviour by police officers. We demonstrate the way in which different policing styles affect the leadership approach best fitted and how this, in turn, affects the way that the police go about tackling their priorities. The chapter demonstrates that good leadership influences the ethical and values culture of an organisation, and therefore is essential to the police service.

Chapter 6 explores how ethics and morals are understood and applied in the use of force by police officers. It considers that, if police are authorised to use force in carrying out their role, how they can ensure that it is deployed reasonably, proportionately, legitimately and only when necessary. The chapter examines some ethical assessment tools for use when police officers have to deploy force during the course of their duty and how they can apply these tools to their decision making.

Chapter 7 highlights that, although a great number of protests take place every year, the majority of these pass peacefully, with police officers being equipped in only their regular uniforms and communicating with the protestors in a peaceful and friendly manner. It is only when protests turn violent or protestors engage in criminality that emphasis on maintaining control rather than enforcing the law becomes paramount. Given the potential confrontational nature of violent protests, where a significant amount of violence and aggression is directly aimed at the police themselves, ethical strategies and tactics that take into consideration human rights, proportionality and accountability are being developed and implemented. The use of ethical decision-making models can not only assist in the development of the strategies, but also offer a tool when commanders have to change tactics as the nature of protests changes in real time.

Chapter 8 explores ethical considerations in relation to covert investigations. It examines the tensions of covert policing, namely the need to obtain information otherwise not available to the police to prevent and detect crime, while respecting the intrusion into the private lives of individuals. The increasing use of legislation to regulate and control covert activities shows that, while it provides some administrative guidance for the police to ensure that they do not act unlawfully or unfairly, it offers very little ethical advice. The chapter provides some ethical decision-making models that can help and support a more ethical approach when considering covert strategies.

Chapter 9 reviews the relationship between policing and corrupt behaviour. It considers how ethics and integrity can help in understanding how deviant behaviour manifests itself both with individual police officers and in police departments. The chapter illustrates that, while the nature and extent of corruption remains elusive, it is accepted that it is a pervasive and continuing problem that occurs at all levels of the police organisation. Moreover, it explores the difficulties concerning how corruption and misconduct are not always clear-cut, giving the example of how gratuities could be seen as either corrupt practice or good community policing. Throughout the chapter, it is acknowledged that deviant behaviour can never be eradicated, but how an ethical framework could assist in helping police officers identify corrupt behaviour and how to respond to it effectively.

Chapter 10 examines how a professional standards culture that has a learning ethos can help inform ethical police strategy and practice. Such a learning culture requires an independent oversight of police misconduct – an independent agency that is empowered with its own investigatory authority. The chapter assesses how the Taylor Review provided the vehicle for a philosophical shift in disciplinary procedures from one based on punishment and sanction to one of learning and responsible behaviour – a change from enforcing a 'disciplinary code' towards a 'code of conduct'. The development of the Independent Police Complaints Commission (IPCC), tasked with independently investigating police complaints, has engendered and supported a learning philosophy in relation to disciplinary procedures, allowing misconduct to be considered within a principled approach to changing the behaviour of the individual.

Chapter 11 focuses on three major issues for the future of policing: the way that the science of policing is offering better-informed options about what works well; the importance of legitimacy and the growing understanding, through research, of its central importance in sustaining effective policing; and the nature and shifting development of democratic principles in policing. We seek to argue throughout this book that ethics and values are a critical golden thread running through good policing. We show just how difficult it is to maintain a consistent ethical approach. Ethical dilemmas in policing are rarely neat and clear-cut. We firmly believe, however, that such dilemmas are better tackled by a workforce for whom ethics are a central part of education and training, and are the everyday currency of their discussions about complex problems.

All chapters follow a similar format. The objectives of the chapter are set out at the beginning, followed by links to the National Occupational Standards (NOS). The chapter then examines a specific ethical policing issue, identifying the key issues and challenges for operational policing. Where appropriate, this includes some discussion on relevant legislation and policy, and how this is applied in practice. The chapter also explores relevant theories of ethics and how these influence policing policy and practice.

This book is intended as an introductory text. Each chapter references and identifies the primary sources of the material used and signposts the reader to further sources of information; there are also practical and reflective tasks in each chapter. These tasks may be undertaken individually, but afford greater learning if they are carried out as tasks for learning sets or seminar groups. This enables the reader to work together with other students, sharing learning and knowledge, as well as from the written material.

REFLECTIVE TASK

- *Why is it important for police officers to understand the importance of ethics and ethical behaviour in carrying out their duties?*

- *What could be some of the challenges in 'doing the right thing' as opposed to 'doing things right'?*

Ethics and philosophy

The principles of ethics and ethical behaviour are found within the discipline of philosophy. The word 'philosophy' is derived from the Greek 'philosophia', which means the love of wisdom (SQA, 2007). It encompasses the pursuit of knowledge by rational inquiry (Caris, 2010).

Philosophy has traditionally covered four main themes.

- *Ethics or moral philosophy – what is the best way to live your life?*

- *Metaphysics – what is the nature of existence and being?*

- *Epistemology – what is knowledge and what does it mean to 'know something'?*

- *Logic – what are the correct principles for rational thought?*

(SQA, 2007, p68)

From these four themes, the one that is most relevant to this book is ethics or moral philosophy. 'Ethics' is another Greek word meaning 'arising from habit', but it is more commonly recognised as a field of philosophy that considers 'the good', moral principles and right actions (SQA, 2007; www.the freedictionary.com).

The study of ethics falls into three categories.

- *Meta ethics – the study of the concept of ethics.*

- *Normative ethics – the study of how to determine ethical values.*

- *Applied ethics – the study of the use of ethical values.*

(SQA, 2007, p69)

Ethical theory and ethical dilemmas

Since the Greeks first applied their thinking to moral issues, different philosophers have provided explanations for ethical behaviour on *either* the importance of *fundamental principles* or the importance of the *consequences of actions* (SQA, 2007, p78). It is these two schools of thought – fundamental principles and consequences of actions – that we will explore in relation to policing, followed by an account of post-modern ethics. The school of philosophy falls into the early Greek philosophers and modern philosophers. For the Greek philosophers, we will look at the work and influence of Plato and Aristotle, and the difference between these two schools of thought. In particular, Aristotle argues that ethics are subjective and relativistic, whereas for Plato they are objective and absolute. These two schools of thought are critical in understanding the complexity of adopting an ethical approach in policing. For the school of modern philosophy we will examine the writings of Immanuel Kant and Jeremy Bentham. The writings of Bauman will be explored in relation to post-modern ethics.

Plato

A wise man speaks because he has something to say; a fool because he has to say something.

(Plato)

Plato (428–348 BC) stated that all people acknowledged and understood the notion of 'good'. People recognised good things, good outcomes and good intentions. He argued that ethical decisions were the ones that were made to achieve 'the good' (SQA, 2007). However, Plato rejected the notion that 'the good' could be defined by pleasure; it was defined by a person acting justly. For a person to act justly they had to have a balance of wisdom, courage and self-control, and evil or bad was due to a lack of knowledge and to ignorance. Therefore, Plato was concerned with how the individual balanced their own state rather than the way they treated other people; if a balance is maintained within each individual, they would treat other people justly. Plato's theory falls into the school of fundamental principles (Vardy and Grosch, 1999).

Aristotle

Even when laws have been written down, they ought not always to remain unaltered.

(Aristotle)

On the other hand, the Greek philosopher Aristotle (384–322 BC) provided an alternative theory. His theory is premised on the consequences of actions and how decisions are made by people in order to achieve a specific action. Aristotle argued that everything a person does is to fulfil or achieve a specific aim. Therefore, he was interested in the consequences of the decisions and their ability to contribute to the individual's life, and those of others (Tredennick, 1976). Aristotle referred to a concept he called the 'doctrine of mean'; what he meant by that was that any virtue lies between two extremes. For example, courage lies between the extremes of rashness and cowardice. Individuals will choose their own point on that continuum and, therefore, the doctrine of the mean accepts that each individual action will be different and will vary (SQA, 2007).

Aristotle's theory of ethics differs from Plato's in that his ethics are relativistic whereas Plato's are absolute. For Plato, ethics are objective, because any person with an appropriate level of knowledge can discover 'the good'. For Aristotle, *ethics are subjective because they are individual and the 'mean' can only be discovered by trial and error* (SQA, 2007, p79).

REFLECTIVE TASK

- *How would Plato explain people who know that working 'for cash in hand' while claiming unemployment benefits is wrong but continue to do it?*

- *If that person had a family and elderly parents to support, could their actions be morally justified?*

- *Aristotle argues for people to aim for a mean or middle position. Is there a middle position on keeping a promise and not keeping a promise, as opposed to Kant's belief that all promises must be kept?*

Immanuel Kant

Science is organized knowledge. Wisdom is organized life.

(Immanuel Kant)

In modern philosophy the notion of 'the good', developed by Plato, was further advanced by the eighteenth-century philosopher Immanuel Kant (1724–1804). He also promoted the significance of principles, in that he stated people should make decisions that are consistent with principles, but that principles are not personal in nature (SQA, 2007). So, for Kant, his concern was not 'the good for human beings', but the fundamental principles of the moral decision. Another aspect of Kant's work is that every person should be treated as a self-determining person and be worthy of respect as an individual. Therefore, everyone should be treated with respect regardless of our own view of them and how they have behaved towards us or other people in the past. He recognised the individual's worth and dignity to other people or, in modern terms, he acknowledged what is now referred to as *human rights* (SQA, 2007, p80).

The second Kantian principle is known as the 'categorical imperative', which means that, if we are faced with an ethical dilemma, we have an absolute duty to do the right thing and make a decision that you would wish everyone else to make in the same circumstances. If this is done, the decision conforms to the categorical imperative and is morally permissible (Vardy and Grosch, 1999).

For Kant, principles are absolute and all decisions must be made within these principles. He did not consider that principles could conflict with each other. Under Kant's theory, a person is moral when acting from a sense of duty and in accordance with agreed principles. Kant's theory is also referred to as 'deontological' ethics or 'non-consequentialism', as it concerns ethics where there are no exceptions to the rules. This raises the issue of discretion in policing. If Kant's theory was applied, discretion would not be applicable as all decisions would be the same in all circumstances (Vardy and Grosch, 1999).

Jeremy Bentham

> *It is vain to talk of the interest of the community, without understanding what is the interest of the individual.*

(Jeremy Bentham)

Jeremy Bentham (1748–1832) developed the work of Aristotle and the consequentialist model: that the consequences of moral decisions are more important than the principles of the decision making. He stated that moral decisions should be taken in order to achieve the *greatest good for the greatest number of people* (SQA, 2007, p81). Thus, the end can justify the means. This school of ethical theory is also referred to Utilitarianism.

For Bentham, when making a decision, the various options are identified and the potential consequences are assessed, and the decision made is the one that achieves the greatest good for the greatest number of people (SQA, 2007). This approach does cause difficulties, as it can be a complex process to assess the range of possible consequences for the number of potential decisions that could be made. In many cases, this process is unworkable and the Utilitarian school proposed that they would agree rules that would apply to society and these rules would be agreed after consideration of the consequences. Once the rule was agreed, day-to-day decisions could be made in accordance with the rule without the requirement for the calculations of the consequences of the various decision options. This has become known as 'Rule Utilitarianism'. This Rule holds that Utilitarianism may first develop a set of principles or rules and, from this, specific acts may or may not be permitted. Many of the reforms in the eighteenth and nineteenth centuries to do with the treatment of criminals were the result of Bentham's philosophy (Hudson, 1983; SQA, 2007).

These theories of ethics can be summarised as in Table 1.1.

Table 1.1 Theories of ethics

	Greek	**Modern**
Principles	Plato	Kant
Consequences	Aristotle	Bentham

Source: Reproduced in part from SQA (2007, p81).

REFLECTIVE TASK

- Do you think Kant's principle of treating suspects with respect and dignity applies if the suspect has allegedly sexually abused children? Is there an ethical basis for denying a convicted paedophile, released upon completion of sentence, the opportunity to live a life in the community without any further restrictions to their liberty?

- How can covert techniques, which arguably involve an element of deceit and compromise, be explained by Kant's principles?

- Consider how Bentham's theory may explain the two tasks above.

Zygmunt Bauman

People who are at the forefront of organisational progress are certainly afraid of sticking to experience, tradition and going by the pattern.

(Zygmunt Bauman)

Zygmunt Bauman (1925–) is a sociologist from Poland and has argued that the challenges of post-modernity create moral dilemmas that the traditional theories cannot resolve. Post-modernity is characterised by uncertainty and insecurity. Bauman draws on the work of Glover (1999), who states that uncertainty has been created because of the difference between technological and moral advancements. Bauman asserts that this has created a separation of deeds and outcomes by distance, time and space, which in turn has created moral uncertainty. The further separation of individuals' actions from the outcomes by the intervention of team actions and role actions enhances that confusion. For example, in a critical incident, Gold and Silver Command make decisions in which the actions from those decisions are carried out by officers at the scene of the incident. So those making the decisions are removed from their implementation of actions. Thus, moral identity has become divided and separated from our moral self.

The pace of change in technological advancement adds to the complexity of ethical dilemmas. In response to these moral challenges, Bauman sets out the key features of 'post-modern ethics'.

- *People are neither 'good' nor 'bad'; they are morally ambivalent. No single, logically coherent code will fit this.*

- *Moral phenomena are inherently non-rational and do not fit utility or rules, which presume one right choice.*

- *Most moral choices are ambiguous and any 'moral' approach taken to extremes will produce an immoral result.*

- *Morality is not universal; one single imposed moral code is immoral.*

- *Morality is irrational. This irrationality can be demonstrated in the conflict between the personal autonomy and the community.*

(Bauman, 1993, cited in Neyroud and Beckley, 2001, p46)

Ethics and values

Each person has a set of underlying 'values', which collectively form their personal value system. Values are the standards and principles that we use to make value judgements. They are the criteria by which we judge people, situations and ideas to be good or bad. It is important to remember that value judgements can be made both consciously and unconsciously (SQA, 2007, p70).

The language of 'values' is important and it is possible to use it to assess the 'fit' between your own personal values and the values of an organisation or of other people (SQA, 2007). For example, the European Code of Police Ethics, which was adopted by the Council of Europe Committee of Experts on Police Ethics and Problems of Policing in September 2001, provides guidance for the governments of the member states of the Council of Europe regarding their internal legislation, practice and codes of conduct for their police (www.epac.at/download/Notes_European_Code_of_Police_Ethics.pdf).

Some of the key words below are contained in this Code of Police Ethics.

Accountability	Impartiality
Awareness	Integrity
Code of conduct	Law and order
Corruption	Liberty
Democracy	Public respect
Ethics	Respect for others
Fairness	Rule of law
Human rights	Training
Human rights awareness	Use of reasonable force

PRACTICAL TASK

- *Make a list of what values are important to you. How does this list compare with the values contained within the European Code of Police Ethics?*

- *Identify the areas where your values are similar and where they are different. Where your values are different, write down the potential challenges or conflict that this may cause you in carrying out your police duties.*

- *Would different cultures and religions have the same set, or similar, values as contained in the European Code of Police Ethics?*

Ethical decision making

How do you know what are ethical decisions and what are not? According to the theories of philosophy, decisions that have an ethical component are decisions that are based on principles and will have consequences. However, some decisions will have a greater ethical component than others, and some ethical decisions will be more complex than others. There is a distinction between personal ethical decisions and professional ethical decisions. Each person has their own personal ethical framework in which they themselves decide what values they will live by, the type of person they are, the type of person they will become and the outcomes they wish to achieve. In making professional ethical decisions, the person is required to decide and perform actions on behalf of the organisation for which they work (Black, 2003).

But policing is complex and requires officers to respond to different incidents and events, each demanding a different set of decisions. One of the challenges for policing is that, on occasions, the decisions made will be both personal and professional. The problem that arises from this is, then, how do you recognise when personal ethics impact upon professional ethics? Consider, for example, that you were responsible for a budget and only had enough money left to resource one operation and had to choose which of the two operations should be undertaken. The decision to commit limited resources to one operation and not another can have a significant impact upon different communities and groups. Yet, as a police officer, you are required to balance the needs of different communities and groups, the priority of the policing problem, pressures coming from the communities and the potential impact of the operations. At the same time, some of these decisions could have a personal implication; for example, you may live in one of the communities, or you may have a stronger personal belief on a particular policing problem. Yet you are required to make the decisions within a professional framework, with honesty and integrity, and in a way that is open and accountable. It must be remembered that the impacts of the decisions and the outcomes are likely to affect the stakeholders in different ways and will express different ethical values.

There are models for ethical decision making, developed for other disciplines, that can be useful tools for ethical decision making in policing. We will consider one such model.

The Potter Box Model for ethical decision making

This model was developed by Jay Black (2003) for consideration in making ethical decisions within the medical profession. It considers six different steps.

1. Define the dilemma.

2. Identify the stakeholders.

3. Develop an accountability system.

4. Compare the alternatives.

5. Implement the decision.

6. Monitor the consequences and develop a policy.

The Potter Box Model, as expanded by Black, can be illustrated in the following case study.

CASE STUDY

The Potter Box Model (as expanded by Black)

You have been called to an incident of domestic violence. You arrive at the house where a female is sitting quietly in the chair with visible bruising to her arms and a small cut on her lip. There are two children who are playing in the garden. The husband states that his wife fell down the stairs. When you ask the wife if this is what happened, she nods her head and quietly answers yes.

1. Define the dilemma

The dilemma is that the injuries sustained to the female were caused either as the result of being assaulted by the husband or by her falling down the stairs.

2. Identify the stakeholders

The stakeholders are you (the police officer), the wife, the husband, the children and the police service.

3. Develop an accountability system

You have a duty to protect the female from any further harm caused by violence from her husband.

You have a duty of care to ensure that she receives appropriate medical assistance if she was injured as a result of falling down the stairs.

You have a duty to arrest the husband if he assaulted his wife.

You have a duty of care to the children to ensure that they are not at risk of harm by either being physically assaulted by their father or witnessing violence between their parents.

You have a duty to yourself and the police force to ensure that the decisions you make are justifiable, accountable and transparent.

4. Compare the alternatives

The alternatives are as follows:

(a) *to remove the male from the house by arresting him on suspicion of domestic violence;*

(b) *to remove the female from the house by calling an ambulance to take her to hospital;*

(c) *to call Social Services in relation to children;*

(d) *to do all of (a), (b) and (c) or a combination of the same;*

(e) *to do nothing.*

5. Implement the decision

From the alternatives available make a decision. You have to account and provide the reasons for why you made that decision and why you did not make any of the alternative decisions.

6. Monitor the consequences and develop a policy

You need to develop a model to monitor your decision. This may be by ensuring that you visit the female when the husband is not at home. It could be that you liaise regularly with agencies that are responsible for domestic violence to see if the family are known to them.

You may develop or comply with a force policy that you adopt a 'positive arrest' strategy for all cases of domestic violence.

So, for Black, ethical decision making was a rational process. The model recognises that a number of logical steps have to be progressed before the decision can be implemented. It provided a logical framework for moral decisions and actions. For Black, the consequences of the decision were as important as the decision process itself.

- *Can you think of an incident in policing where there could be competing definitions or explanations for the dilemma or incident as in the case study above?*

- *How would the differing definitions affect the rest of the decision-making process?*

The police have also developed an ethical decision-making model, where every decision is made within the policing mission, values, risk and protecting human rights framework (ACPO, 2011). See Figure 1.1 overleaf.

Types of ethical decisions

There are different types of ethical decisions. Romanelli (1972), a philosopher, considered ethical decisions in relation to medical ethics. He proposed a model for ethical dilemmas, known as the tripartite typology of moral conflict.

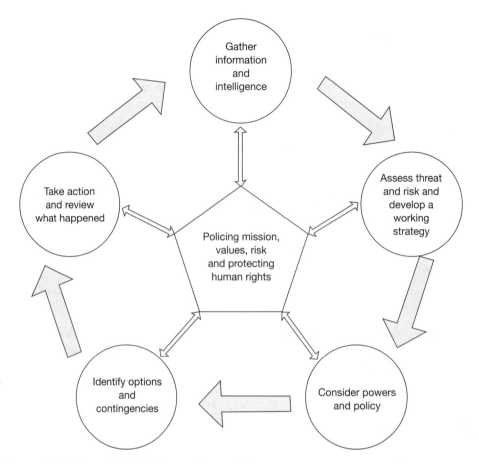

Figure 1.1 Police ethical decision-making model

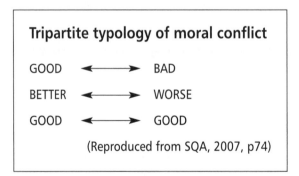

Romanelli recognised that, at level one, there are moral dilemmas where the options are between good and bad. An example of this: if a man attacked another for no reason, causing significant injury, as a moral conflict this is represented as a top-level ethical dilemma, where it is bad to injure a stranger without any moral justification and it would be good not to injure a stranger.

Another level of Romanelli's model recognises that there are ethical dilemmas where the options available each represent 'the good'. An example of this is where you are first on the scene of two people who are trapped in a fire. You can only rescue one of them. One is a mother with two young children and the other is a renowned heart surgeon. You are required to make a decision to save either the mother or the surgeon. Therefore, you have to make the best decision you can, but also recognise that you may not be able to achieve both 'goods' within that decision. This has been referred to as *the tragic problem of the good* (SQA, 2007, p75).

In the middle of Romanelli's model is the ethical dilemma between better and worse. Consider, for example, that you are called to a domestic violence incident. You have to make a decision as to whether to arrest the alleged perpetrator and the decision is made more difficult as the alleged victim is denying any assault, despite having bruising on her arms and face. If you decide to arrest the alleged perpetrator you may make the situation better, in that the perpetrator won't repeat the offence, or you may make the situation worse, in that the perpetrator may increase the severity of the domestic violence once he is released and the victim will become too afraid to report it next time to the police.

Romanelli also referred to the concept of 'rigoristic fallacy'. This is where ethical dilemmas are wrongly classified in accordance with the three levels of the model. It would be a rigoristic fallacy to present someone with an ethical dilemma as though it were a simple decision between 'good and bad', when in fact it was a 'tragic problem of the good' (SQA, 2007). For example, you only have one police car at your disposal, yet you have to make a decision about whether to send the car to an incident involving a vulnerable missing child or to an incident where a serious assault is taking place. Both equally require the immediate attention of the police and it would be equally good to send the car to both, but there are not the resources to do so. It would be wrong to present this as a 'good and bad' level, although it may be possible to see how people could perceive this.

If you were the person to whom the police car was sent, you would perceive it as a good decision. If you were the person to whom the car was not deployed, you would perceive the decision as a bad decision. Therefore, it is important to consider these outcomes when using the ethical decision-making process (SQA, 2007).

Ethics and discretion

Police officers constantly have to make decisions about how they are going to act and respond to situations while they go about their duties. One of the distinctive aspects of policing is that each situation requires a different response; no two situations are the same. Real-time decision making has to be made by officers as they respond and react to the event. Thus, the very purpose of a code of ethics is to provide a framework, and by default accountability, for the decision-making process.

All situations require an ethical response, but some have a more obvious ethical response than others. For example, a police officer responds to a call from a neighbour of a family who is concerned that the children are being abused. When the police officer arrives at the house where the children live, he finds that two young children aged six and eight years have been locked in the bedroom. The father states that he has locked them in the bedroom as they have been naughty. The mother of the children sits very quietly in the corner, not willing to say anything. The police officer has to make a set of decisions that are highly charged and emotional. As the police officer leaves the premises, he notices that the car of the neighbour who reported the incident has an outdated tax disc. He also has to make a decision about this, but it is not so highly charged or emotional as the ones he has just made. Nonetheless, the decisions he makes for both issues will have a considerable impact upon how the individuals involved view the police. Ethics and discretion will be discussed more fully in Chapters 2 and 3.

CHAPTER SUMMARY

This chapter outlined why ethics are integral to policing policy and practice. It has given you an introduction to philosophy and, in particular, ethical theory and ethical dilemmas by examining the Greek and modern theories of ethics. The chapter has also introduced you to ethical decision making and what informs personal and professional ethical decisions. Finally, the chapter examined the different types of ethical decisions and provided models for making such decisions.

FURTHER READING

Much of the reading in this chapter is from various sources drawing upon a range of disciplines. However, Peter Neyroud and Alan Beckley's book, *Policing Ethics and Human Rights* (2001), provides a comprehensive overview of ethics in policing, linking it both to recent developments and the human rights agenda.

Professor John Kleinig's book *The Ethics of Policing* (1996) offers a comprehensive and philosophical discussion of police ethics. It examines both personal and professional ethics and sets these within organisational ethics.

REFERENCES

ACPO (Association of Chief Police Officers) The National Decision Model. Presented at the Higher Education Forum for Police Learning and Development, University of Northampton, 6 September 2011.

Aristotle (1943 edition) *Nicomachean Ethics*. New York: Walter J Black.

Black, J (2003) *Media Ethics: Between Iraq and a hard place*. Honors Excellence Occasional Papers Series, vol. II, no. 2. Miami, FL: Florida International University.

Caris, C (2010) Personal communication, 12 June 2010.

Glover, J (1999) *Humanity: A moral history of the twentieth century*. London: Jonathan Cope.

Hudson, P (1983) The Crime Victim and the Criminal Justice System: Time for a change. New York: Basic Books.

Kleinig, J (1996) *The Ethics of Policing,* Cambridge: Cambridge University Press.

Neyroud, P and Beckley, A (2001) *Policing, Ethics and Human Rights*. Cullompton: Willan.

Pollock, J (1998) *Ethics in Crime and Justice.* Belmont, CA: Wadsworth.

Romanelli, P (1972) Medical Ethics in Philosophical Perspective, in Visscher, M (ed.) *Humanistic Approaches in Medical Ethics*. London: Pemberton Books.

SQA (Scottish Qualifications Authority) (2007) *PDA Diploma in Police Service Leadership and Management: Professional ethics in policing*, CB3740. Glasgow: SQA.

Tredennick, H (1976) *Ethics.* London: Penguin Classics.

Vardy, P and Grosch, P (1999) *The Puzzle of Ethics.* London: HarperCollins.

USEFUL WEBSITES

www.acpo.police.uk – Association of Chief Police Officers

www.acpos.police.uk – Association of Chief Police Officers in Scotland

www.homeoffice.gov.uk – Home Office

www.justice.gov.uk – Ministry of Justice

www.nipolicingboard.org.uk/publications/final_code_of_ethics-2.pdf – code of ethics for the Police Service Northern Ireland

www.skillsforjustice-nosfinder.com – Skills for Justice, National Occupational Standards

www.sqa.org.uk/sqa/33667.html – Scottish Qualifications Authority PDA Diploma in Police Service Leadership and Management: Professional ethics in policing

2 Professional policing and a code of ethics

Introduction

Historically, there were considered to be only three professions – the clergy, medical doctors and lawyers – and it was only members of these occupations who held the monopoly on professional status and on professional education (Perks, 1993). However, in the nineteenth century, there was an increase in occupational specialisation and other occupations began to develop 'professional' status, such as accountants, engineers and pharmacists. This aspiration for occupations to achieve professional status remained unabated so that many occupational groups have now become recognised as professions. There is also recognition that many occupations do not qualify for professional status.

PRACTICAL TASK

- *List four professions and four occupations.*

- *What are the differences between a profession and an occupation?*

Policing as a profession

There has been much debate about whether policing is a profession or an occupation. The Neyroud Report (2010), *Review of Police Leadership and Training*, purported that, for policing to be effective, it needed to move from being a service that acts professionally to becoming a profession. Traditionally, policing was considered a blue-collar occupation and recruited primarily from the working-class community (Reiner, 1992). In part, this stems from policing at first being based on a military model, making it a hierarchical and disciplined occupation. This gave rise to a rank-and-file structure with an ethos that reflected a uniformed organisation with a regime of drill and saluting, and a unique occupational culture. This culture has been characterised by the following traits: conservatism, masculinity, homogeneity and the fostering of 'us and them' leading to separatism (Dunivin, 1994; Reiner, 1992). Such characteristics are associated with an occupation and not a profession.

However, since the 1980s, the notion of policing as a working-class occupation has been increasingly challenged, together with both the role and function of the police (Alderson, 1998). This has led to calls for the police to become a professional organisation. Bullock and Trombley describe this transformation process thus:

> A profession arises when any trade or occupation transforms itself through the development of formal qualifications based upon education, apprenticeship, and examinations, the emergence of regulatory bodies with powers to admit and discipline members, and some degree of monopoly rights.
>
> (Bullock and Trombley, 1999, p689)

Therefore, a profession can be defined as a vocation founded upon specialised and extensive educational training (Webb and Webb, 1917).

Defining a profession

There are numerous definitions of what a profession is. For example, the *Shorter Oxford Dictionary* (1970) defines a profession as:

> *The occupation to which one professes to be skilled in and to follow. A vocation in which a professed knowledge of some department of learning is used in its application to the affairs of others, or in the practice of an art founded upon it.*

The Australian Council of Professions defines a profession as:

> *A disciplined group of individuals who adhere to high ethical standards and uphold themselves to, and are accepted by, the public as possessing special knowledge and skills in a widely recognised, organised body of learning derived from education and training at high level, and who are prepared to exercise this knowledge and these skills in the interests of others. Inherent in this definition is the concept that the responsibility for the welfare, health and safety of the community shall take precedence over other considerations.*
>
> (ACCC, 2011)

It is important to note that, while certain occupations are referred to as professions, a profession is always held by the individual and not the organisation that they work for. The status of profession is generally that person's way of generating an income. Perks (1993) purports that a professional normally has to be licensed and regulated by a self-regulated association of that profession. In order for an individual to become licensed, they must receive a higher level of education and pass examinations. Professionals are subject to a code of conduct that they agree to uphold as part of the licensing process. Failure to adhere to the professional code of conduct can result in the individual being disciplined, and their licence to practise revoked. Generally, people without licences are prohibited by law from engaging in those activities practised by professionals.

Characteristics of a profession

If there is no agreed universally accepted definition of a profession, it is then useful to consider the requirements and characteristics for an occupation to become a profession. Bryant and Bryant (2009) identify five key requirements for a profession.

- A body of knowledge and higher level theory underpinning the practice of the profession.

- Control or regulation on entry to the profession by a professional association.

- Autonomy, discretion and a degree of self-regulation normally exercised by the professional association.

- The profession is underpinned by vocational practice.

- The profession has a code of ethics.

PRACTICAL TASK

- *Using the five requirements for a profession listed on p20, identify which of the criteria the police service meets in order to satisfy these requirements.*

- *Now identify which criteria the police service does not fulfil to meet the requirements for a profession.*

The five requirements identified on p20 can be further considered by examining the characteristics of a profession. Perks (1993, pp2–14) identifies a range of characteristics that help define a profession.

1. **Skill based on theoretical knowledge**: Professionals are assumed to have extensive theoretical knowledge and to possess skills based on that knowledge that they are able to apply in practice.

2. **Professional association**: Professions usually have professional bodies organised by their members, which are intended to enhance the status of their members and have carefully controlled entrance requirements.

3. **Extensive period of education**: The most prestigious professions usually require at least three years at university.

4. **Testing of competence**: Before being admitted to membership of a professional body, there is a requirement to pass prescribed examinations that are based on mainly theoretical knowledge.

5. **Institutional training**: In addition to examinations, there is usually a requirement for a long period of institutionalised training where aspiring professionals acquire specified practical experience in some sort of trainee role before being recognised as a full member of a professional body. Continuous upgrading of skills through professional development is also mandatory.

6. **Licensed practitioners**: Professions seek to establish a register or membership so that only those individuals so licensed are recognised as bona fide.

7. **Work autonomy**: Professionals tend to retain control over their work, even when they are employed outside the profession in commercial or public organisations.

8. **Code of professional conduct or ethics**: Professional bodies usually have codes of conduct or ethics for their members and disciplinary procedures for those who infringe the rules.

9. **Self-regulation**: Professional bodies tend to be self-regulating and independent from government. Professions tend to be policed and regulated by senior, respected practitioners and the most highly qualified members of the profession.

10. **Legitimacy**: Professions have clear legal authority over some activities (e.g. upholding and enforcing the law), but are also seen as adding legitimacy to a wide range of related activities.

11. **Inaccessible body of knowledge**: In some professions, the body of knowledge is relatively inaccessible to the uninitiated. Medicine and law are typically not school subjects and have separate faculties and even separate libraries at universities.

REFLECTIVE TASK

- *Do you consider the police service to be an occupation or a profession?*

- *Should the police service be a profession or an occupation? Explain your answer.*

It has been argued that there are advantages of the police service striving to become recognised as a profession. The reasons put forward include that it would ensure that, as an organisation, the police service would develop and maintain a body of knowledge that is academically rigorous and underpins vocational practice. It would further allow for the police service to set up its own professional association that will enable it to have greater regulation, autonomy and discretion.

Police discretion, autonomy and self-regulation

Police officers and police staff are empowered with significant police discretion and autonomy in carrying out their operational duties. The high level of discretion afforded to police officers is essential to the practice of policing. As Lord Scarman noted:

> the exercise of discretion lies at the heart of the policing function. It is undeniable that there is only one law for all: and it is right that this should be so. But it is equally well recognized that successful policing depends on the exercise of discretion on how the law is enforced . . . Discretion is the art of suiting action to particular circumstances.
>
> (Scarman, 1981, quoted in Bryant and Bryant, 2009, p124)

So, if discretion is, as Lord Scarman defines, the art of exercising how the law is enforced in any particular situation, it follows that two people committing the same offence may have very different outcomes. Consider if Mr A and Mr B independently committed the same offence. In the case of Mr A, the police officer gave a verbal warning, but Mr B was arrested and a charge was brought against him.

Mr B has no grounds for complaint as he has committed the offence and therefore is subject to the full weight of the sanction. Yet, if one person is subjected to the full weight of punishment for committing the offence, why do not all persons deserve to be given the same punishment?

REFLECTIVE TASK

Mr A and Mr B were both stopped in the street in Newtown in separate incidents for identical behaviour – being drunk and disorderly in a public place. In the case of Mr A, Police Officer Smith gave him a verbal warning and instructed him to go home. However, on encountering Mr B, Police Officer Smith arrested him, took him back to the police station and issued formal charges.

- *Should all people be given the same punishment for committing the same crime?*

- *What reasons can you give for the police issuing different forms of punishment for different people committing the same crime?*

- *Which do you consider to be most unfair: that Mr A is not subject to the full sanction of the law or that Mr B is subject to the full sanction of the law?*

- *Can discretion lead to unfair behaviour by police officers?*

- *What are the implications for removing police discretion in relation to a professional policing organisation?*

As we can conclude, although discretion may be a vital element of policing, it does present problems for a self-regulating profession.

While police officers are empowered to exercise discretion, the foundation of the police service is based on autonomy. The notion that the police service should be free from political interference and that each constabulary should retain the traditional ideal of independence is a key principle of British policing (Oliver, 1987). This has meant that police groups such as ACPO, the Police Superintendents' Association and the Police Federation play a powerful role in directing police policy and practice. Collectively, these groups can form a powerful lobbying body against undue political pressure. For example, they managed to prevent a controversial reform related to performance-related pay and structural changes in the early 1990s (Leishman et al., 1996). In addition, ACPO would also assert that it strives to ensure a high-quality and professional service. The idea of police enjoying high degrees of professional independence has, however, been subject to criticism by academics and policy commentators, who argue that too much independence for the police conflicts with accountability to democratic control (Sklansky, 2011).

However, while these groups, both individually and collectively, may fulfil some of the responsibilities of a professional association, they are not professional associations. You may recall that two of the requirements for a profession were as follows.

- Control or regulation on entry to the profession by a professional association.

- Autonomy, discretion and a degree of self-regulation normally exercised by the professional association.

Professional associations, therefore, are empowered with a high degree of self-regulation.

As Kleinig (1996) asserts, self-regulation in professions causes members to believe that only members of that profession are the best people to pass judgement on the quality of their services. Professions such as medicine and law claim that the uniqueness of their roles and services means that only they can fully understand why certain actions and conduct need to be taken. For the police service to become a profession, it would mean that it establishes its own professional association to act as a self-regulating body. However, self-regulation may be more difficult for the police service. The following case study illustrates some of the potential challenges for the police service in achieving self-regulation.

CASE STUDIES

In 1999, Her Majesty's Inspectorate of Constabulary (HMIC) undertook an inspection on integrity within the police service. The inspection examined issues of fairness, behaviour, probity and a range of management and operational issues. The report highlighted a number of issues relating to the integrity of the police service. One area of concern related to 'administrative corruption', where police officers altered or manipulated police data in order to enhance performance. Other areas of concern included the lack of personal integrity among officers and ways of training in relation to encouraging officers to act with integrity. The report stated:

> Ethical personnel strategies are essential in maintaining high levels of integrity; these should start at the initial recruitment stage where, in many cases, the Inspection discovered a lack of robust systems. Much more could be done, such as more vigorous vetting, drug testing etc. The quality of tutor constables is the vital element in setting probationers off along the right road and if their selection and training is found wanting, there is a greater risk that a lack of integrity will develop in new recruits.
>
> *(HMIC, 1999, p4)*

In the same year as the HMIC report, Sir William Macpherson (1999) published his report into the death of Stephen Lawrence. The report severely criticised the Metropolitan Police Service for failing to adequately investigate the murder of Stephen, a black teenager, in 1993. In his report, Sir William identified the police service as being professionally incompetent and institutionally racist.

In 2003, the BBC aired a documentary, The Secret Policeman, *which showed an undercover investigative journalist who joined the police service to gain an insider view of police training. He exposed extreme racist attitudes by some police student officers and a culture that was not open to challenging racist and unacceptable behaviour.*

The cases above demonstrate the need for the police service to be open to public scrutiny and the need for mechanisms to be able to recognise, acknowledge and effectively self-regulate deviant and poor behaviour and practice.

The Macpherson Inquiry was a key influence in the development of the Independent Police Complaints Commission (IPCC). The IPCC was set up to provide an autonomous police complaints system independent from police and political interference.

If issues of police discretion and autonomy present unique challenges as the police move towards becoming a profession, there have been significant developments in defining a code of ethics for the police service. Although, as we shall see later in this chapter, some police forces have codes of ethics, these have not been adopted by all forces. However, there has been a promotion of core standards through the adoption by most police forces of a Statement of Common Purpose and Values that police officers should adhere to, which incorporates a code of conduct.

Codes of ethics

Many professions have codes of ethics in which members agree to accept and be bound by certain rules and standards as they enter the profession. Thus a code of ethics is a set of statements that represents the profession's collective moral values and beliefs. It is a set of principles or standards that provides a framework of acceptable behaviour for members of that profession and allows members to consider their conduct, behaviour and actions as they carry out their occupational duties. A code of ethics can also increase public confidence in organisations as it demonstrates that members of the profession are committed to working within an ethical framework while discharging their duties.

A formal code of ethics provides a framework and understanding of the behaviours, actions and ideals that both individuals and the organisation aspire to. Therefore, it will establish a point of reference for both the organisation and members of the organisation for acceptable behaviour in carrying out their professional duties. This point of reference will address a number of criteria, which may vary from one code to another but generally include six key conditions.

1. A code of ethics provides a definition of acceptable behaviours to which the members of that profession must adhere and conform.

2. A code of ethics promotes the highest standards of practice by the members of that profession while undertaking professional practice.

3. A code of ethics establishes a framework of professional behaviour, responsibility, accountability and compliance.

4. There are sanctions for members of the profession who do not comply or conform to the conditions detailed in the code of conduct. This can include being banned from practising the profession.

5. A code of ethics represents the occupational identity for the profession as well as defining public expectation required from members of the profession in carrying out their professional duties.

6. A formal code of ethics identifies the occupation as a profession that has acquired professional maturity.

While a code of ethics defines consideration of professional conduct by individual members, it can also provide the basis for establishing the merit of a formal complaint against a member of the profession (Neyroud, 2008). Thus, the performance and conduct of a member of the profession can be measured against the code of ethics. Therefore, a code of ethics can be described as a tool to ensure the decision making and behaviour of individual members is of the highest integrity and value.

REFLECTIVE TASK

- List three occupations that have codes of ethics and three occupations that do not.

- Consider if all occupations should have a code of ethics. What would be the advantages and disadvantages of the police service having a code of ethics?

The oath of office

As they join the service, every police officer has to swear an oath of office before a magistrate. The oath of office provides a set of standards and values for police officers concerning the way they are expected to carry out their duties.

The oath of office

I, ... of ...... do solemnly and sincerely declare and affirm that I will well and truly serve the Queen in the office of constable, with fairness, integrity, diligence and impartiality, upholding fundamental human rights and according equal respect to all people; and that I will, to the best of my power, cause the peace to be kept and preserved and prevent all offences against people and property; and that while I continue to hold the said office I will to the best of my skill and knowledge discharge all the duties thereof faithfully according to law.

(Police Act 2002, s83)

Statement of Common Purpose and Values

In 1993, ACPO, in an attempt to establish a set of principles for professional behaviour for the police service, issued a Statement of Common Purpose and Values. This document emphasised the importance of providing quality of service to the public by police officers undertaking their duties with fairness, integrity and impartiality. While police forces signed up to this Statement of Common Purpose and Values, its influence was limited.

Code of Conduct

The Police Act 1996 introduced a Code of Conduct, which came into operation in 1999, as a response to concerns about the police disciplinary process. This Code of Conduct introduced new misconduct procedures that replaced the existing police regulations. The Code focuses on a framework for punishment of poor behaviour and performance, which

Neyroud and Beckley (2001) have argued is not a substitute for the development of a positive and full statement of ethics to deliver good professional standards. The Code of Conduct, despite its objectives, has also been criticised for its lack of independence by police associations.

Current arrangements for professional behaviour

- Oath of office (officers attested on commencement of service).
- Statement of Common Purpose and Values (ACPO, 1999).
- Code of Conduct (Police Act 1996).

The development of a code of ethics

It has been argued that a rigid code of ethics for the police service could be restrictive and not allow police officers to exercise their powers in certain conditions. But a code of ethics need not be as rigid as to work against the natural principles and justice of policing; rather a code should assist and direct ethical decision making and behaviour (Black, 2003; SQA, 2007). Neyroud and Beckley go further in their assertion for a code of ethics for policing and identify four major reasons as to why such a code is not just desirable, but necessary.

- *The introduction of the Humans Rights Act 1998 and the Freedom of Information Act 2000 will fundamentally reform the nature of policing, bringing a new focus towards ethical behaviour by police officers.*
- *The increasing trend towards accountability and liability of actions by both police officers and the police organization.*
- *Growing public concern over police actions.*
- *Lack of confidence in the police by the communities they police.*

(2001, p193)

The first code of ethics for police can be traced back to the Universal Declaration on Human Rights (UDHR) in 1948. This Declaration was written by countries sharing a common heritage of political traditions, ideals, freedom and the rule of law, but it applies to any country that signs and ratifies the Declaration (Pike, 1985; SQA, 2007).

In 1963, the United Nations Committee on Crime Prevention and Control started to develop a police ethics code, but this was not to be completed and adopted until 1979 (SQA, 2007). In the same year, the Council of Europe issued a European Declaration on the Police. This Declaration was based on the principle of maintaining high standards of behaviour within the police to preserve the human rights of the individual members of society that they policed (polis.osce.org/library/view?item_id=2687&attach_id=500).

The first code of ethics for policing in the United Kingdom was contained in the draft 'Principles of Policing' issued by ACPO in 1992, but even though this code of ethics was widely circulated it was not taken up or introduced as police protocol. However, more recently, the Police Service of Northern Ireland (PSNI) drew up a Code of Ethics and this was defined in Section 52 of the Police (Northern Ireland) Act 2000. There were ten articles contained within this Code of Ethics, and these took account of the European Convention on Human Rights and the relevant United Nations standards, to reflect best practice in ethical policing.

Code of Ethics for the Police Service of Northern Ireland

Article 1: Professional Duty
Article 2: Police Investigations
Article 3: Privacy and Confidentiality
Article 4: Use of Force
Article 5: Detained Persons
Article 6: Equality
Article 7: Integrity
Article 8: Property
Article 9: Fitness for Duty
Article10: Duty of Supervisors

(Reproduced with permission from SQA, 2007, pp109–10)

The Code of Ethics also acts as a disciplinary code for police officers in the PSNI for behaviour both on and off duty. Compliance with the Code of Ethics is mandatory and all police officers are legislatively bound by its provisions. The Code has been linked to police officers' annual performance reviews (SQA, 2007).

In 2007, the Association of Chief Police Officers in Scotland (ACPOS) published a Statement of Ethical Principles.

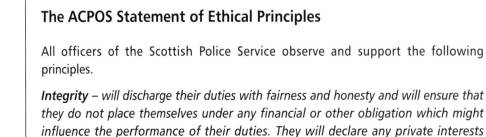

The ACPOS Statement of Ethical Principles

All officers of the Scottish Police Service observe and support the following principles.

Integrity *– will discharge their duties with fairness and honesty and will ensure that they do not place themselves under any financial or other obligation which might influence the performance of their duties. They will declare any private interests which may conflict with their duties and take steps to avoid such conflict.*

Transparency – *will perform their duties in an open and transparent nature, submit their decisions and actions to appropriate scrutiny and will respond positively to criticism. They will give reasons for their decisions and restrict information only when the wider public interest demands. They will be open and truthful about their actions while maintaining the confidentiality of information entrusted to them in accordance with the law.*

Accountability – *will remain accountable before the law and accept responsibility for their decisions and actions. They will guard against the abuse of powers which their office affords them and will oppose and draw attention to malpractice and wrongdoing by others.*

Responsibility – *will accept personal responsibility for their own actions and omissions and act with resolve, tolerance and restraint in the discharge of their duties. They will ensure that their actions are at all times lawful, reasonable and proportionate and take ownership of those actions and decisions made in the course of their duties. They will take responsibility for observance of these principles and promote them through leadership and personal example.*

Impartiality – *will act fairly and impartially, without prejudice and solely in terms of the public interest. They will discharge their duties with objectivity and without favour or malice.*

In addition, the Statement of Ethical Principles addresses another five key features that are not ethical issues as such, but relate more to expected and acceptable standards of conduct. These are as follows.

- *Employee's responsibilities*
  - *Conduct out of hours*
  - *Associations*
  - *Use of facilities*
  - *Disclosure of criminal convictions and road traffic convictions*
  - *Conduct during working hours*
  - *Confidentiality*
  - *Use of discretion*
  - *Discriminatory behaviour*
  - *Reporting corruption*
  - *Vetting*

- *Management responsibilities*

- *Gifts and hospitality*

- *Declaration of interests*
  - *Use of warrant cards*
  - *Charitable events*

- *Substance misuse*

(www.scotland.gov.uk/Publications/2004/06/19502/38836)

Following on from the ACPOS Statement of Ethical Principles, ACPO published a Code of Ethics, adopting the Nolan Principles, which relate to duties and responsibilities of those holding public office. Lord Nolan began the first report of his committee on standards in public life by setting out what he referred to as 'The seven principles of public life'.

The ACPO Code of Ethics (Nolan Principles)

Selflessness – *Holders of public office should take decisions solely in terms of the public interest. They should not do so in order to gain financial or other material benefits for themselves, their family, or their friends.*

Integrity – *Holders of public office should not place themselves under any financial or other obligations to outside individuals or organisations that might influence them in the performance of their official duties.*

Objectivity – *In carrying out public business, including making public appointments, awarding contracts, or recommending individuals for rewards or benefits, holders of public office should make choices on merit.*

Accountability – *Holders of public office are accountable for their decisions and actions to the public and must submit themselves to whatever scrutiny is appropriate to their office.*

Openness – *Holders of public office should be seen [to be] as open as possible about all the decisions and actions that they take. They should give reasons for their decisions and restrict information only when a wider public interest clearly demands.*

Honesty – *Holders of public office have a duty to declare any private interests relating to their public duties and to take steps to resolve any conflicts arising in a way that protects the public interest.*

Leadership – *Holders of public office should promote and support these principles by leadership and example.*

(www.acpo.police.uk)

REFLECTIVE TASK

- *Consider the various codes of ethics as set out by the PSNI, ACPOS and ACPO. What are the similarities and do any of the codes have unique ethical principles that the others do not?*

- *How can a code of ethics assist in raising the standards of policing for a police officer?*

It has been argued that the development of a code of ethics is one of the characteristics of a profession, and thus Pike (1985) has argued that the emergence of a code of ethics demonstrates that policing is developing into a 'profession'. But one has to ask whether, even if a code of ethics is introduced, will it bring the desired benefits? The merits of introducing a code of ethics have been keenly debated. While some commentators have suggested that a code of ethics will not necessarily professionalise the police service, others conclude that a code of ethics would:

- improve public perception of the police;
- improve public confidence and trust;
- develop and support police officers' personal moral conduct;
- reduce unethical behaviour in the police service;
- bring an awareness of ethical decision making and its implications into police actions;
- improve the quality of the police service in communities.

C H A P T E R   S U M M A R Y

This chapter examined the requirements and characteristics of a profession and how these can be applied to the police service. It explored the issues of police autonomy and police discretion in relation to self-regulation. The chapter also introduced codes of ethics and conduct and current arrangements for the police. Finally, the chapter considered the benefits of a code of ethics for the police service.

FURTHER READING

Much of the chapter draws on different chapters from a range of books; however, a useful report to read in conjunction with this chapter is the *Review of Police Leadership and Training Report* by Peter Neyroud (2010).

REFERENCES

ACCC (Australian Competition & Consumer Commission) (2011) Definition of a Profession. Online at www.accc.gov.au/content/index/phtml/itemId/277772 (accessed 15 November 2011).

ACPO (Association of Chief Police Officers) (1999) *The Human Rights Audit Tool*. London: ACPO.

Alderson, J (1998) *Principled Policing: Protecting the public with integrity*. Winchester: Waterside Press.

Black, J (2003) *Media Ethics: Between Iraq and a hard place*. Honors Excellence Occasional Papers Series, vol. II, No. 2. Miami, FL: Florida International University.

Bryant, R and Bryant, S (eds) (2009) *Student Police Officer Handbook 2010*. Oxford: Oxford University Press.

Bullock, A and Trombley, S (1999) *The New Fontana Dictionary of Modern Thought*. London: HarperCollins.

Dunivin, K (1994) Military Culture: Change and continuity. *Armed Forces and Culture*, 20(4): 531–47.

HMIC (Her Majesty's Inspectorate of Constabulary) (1999) *Police Integrity: Securing and maintaining public confidence.* London: HMIC.

Kleinig, J (1996) *The Ethics of Policing.* Cambridge: Cambridge University Press.

Leishman, F, Cope, S and Starie, P (1996) *Police Reform in Britain.* Politics Review, pp.19–22.

Macpherson, Sir William (1999) *Report of the Stephen Lawrence Inquiry.* London: HMSO.

Neyroud, P (2008) Past, Present and Future Performance: Lessons and prospects for the management of police performance. *Policing*, 2: 340–9.

Neyroud, P (2010) *Review of Police Leadership and Training Report.* London: Home Office.

Neyroud, P and Beckley A (2001) *Policing, Ethics and Human Rights.* Cullompton: Willan.

Oliver, I (1987) *Police Government and Accountability.* London: Macmillan.

Perks, RW(1993) *Accounting and Society.* London: Chapman & Hall.

Pike, M (1985) *The Principles of Policing.* London: Macmillan.

Reiner, R (1992) Police Research in the United Kingdom: A critical review, in Tonry, M and Morris, N (eds) *Modern Policing.* Chicago, IL: University of Chicago Press.

Sklansky, DA (2011) Private Policing and Human Rights. *Law and Ethics of Human Rights*, 5(1): article 3.

SQA (Scottish Qualifications Authority) (2007) *PDA Diploma in Police Service Leadership and Management: Professional ethics in policing*, CB3740. Glasgow: SQA.

Webb, S and Webb, B (1917) *Architect Services.* Quoted in the New Statements at paragraph 123 of a report by the UK Competition Commission, dated 8 November 1977.

USEFUL WEBSITES

www.acpo.police.uk – Association of Chief Police Officers

www.acpos.police.uk – Association of Chief Police Officers in Scotland

www.homeoffice.gov.uk – Home Office

www.ipcc.gov.uk/index/complainants/who_complaint/pol_codeconduct.htm – Independent Police Complaints Commission and the police Code of Conduct

www.justice.gov.uk – Ministry of Justice

www.nipolicingboard.org.uk/final_code_of_ethics-2.pdf – Code of Ethics for the Police Service Northern Ireland

www.polis.osce.org/library/view?item_id=2687&attach_id=500 – European Code of Police Ethics and the European Declaration on the Police

www.skillsforjustice-nosfinder.com – Skills for Justice, National Occupational Standards

www.sqa.org.uk/sqa/33667.html – Scottish Qualifications Authority PDA Diploma in Police Service Leadership and Management: Professional ethics in policing

3 Police culture and ethical policing

CHAPTER OBJECTIVES

By the end of this chapter you should be able to:

- understand different theories of police culture and how these theories relate to police behaviour and values;
- appreciate the influence of police culture on the police organisation, police officers and society;
- understand how police discretion can affect police behaviour through cultural norms;
- appreciate how ethics can inform and influence police culture.

LINKS TO STANDARDS

This chapter provides opportunities for links with the following Skills for Justice, National Occupational Standards (NOS) for Policing and Law Enforcement 2008.

AE1.1 Maintain and develop your own knowledge, skills and competence.
CA1 Use law enforcement actions in a fair and justified way.
HA1 Manage your own resources.
HA2 Manage your own resources and professional development.
HA15 Provide information to support decision making.
HB4 Provide leadership in your area of responsibility.

With the introduction of the Qualification and Credit Framework (QCF), it is likely that the term 'National Occupational Standards' will change. At the time of writing it is not clear what the new title will be, although it is known that some organisations will use the term 'QCF assessment units'.

Links to current NOS are provided at the start of each chapter; however, it should be noted that these are currently subject to review and it is recommended that you visit the Skills for Justice website to check the currency of all the NOS provided: www.skillsforjustice-nosfinder.com.

Introduction

The police possess a distinctive culture that is characterised by the beliefs, behaviour, thinking and interaction that police officers share in common. 'Police culture' thus refers to the combination of values, attitudes, prejudices and working practices found among police officers (Waddington, 2008). Foster (2003) has argued that cultural factors influence and shape how policing is defined and determine police priorities and practice. This chapter examines how the culture of the police differs from other organisational cultures and its significance in ethical behaviour and practice.

Police discretion – how the police selectively apply the law in various situations – is also considered in relation to culture. The wide degree of discretion afforded to police officers has often been linked to the more negative features of police culture. This chapter explores how police discretion can facilitate or challenge deviant or corrupt police behaviour.

Organisational cultures

All organisations have their own cultures and, in most cases, this is not seen as a negative or harmful feature. However, police culture is often presented as a damaging attribute of policing because of the more negative characteristics associated with it. Organisational culture does affect the way in which members of that organisation perceive and interpret their function and role. This is particularly significant for police officers, whose role often involves being exposed to uncertain and unpredictable situations, sometimes with an element of danger (Foster, 2003).

PRACTICAL TASK

- *List two occupations other than policing that are male-dominated and two that are predominantly female.*

- *Are the cultures of these gendered occupations perceived as being significantly different?*

Morgan (1992) argues that a significant feature of an organisational culture is its gender quality. Traditionally male-dominated occupations, such as the army, air force, fire and prison services, are characterised as being close-knit organisations and exclusive to those members. Gregory and Lees (1999) argue that male bonding in male-dominated organisations develops a supportive trust network that is required when responding to difficult and dangerous situations. However, this bonding process can result in hostile and exclusionary behaviour towards people who are not part of that organisation. Moreover, this hostile and exclusionary behaviour can manifest itself within other groups of the organisation that are perceived to be different from each other (Foster, 2003). Foster further asserts that these inequalities often *reflect, reinforce and sometimes amplify broader structural inequalities in society* (Foster, 2003, p197). Characteristics inherent in organisational cultures are rarely articulated in formal policy or statements of the organisation, thus there are fundamental differences in how the organisation presents itself formally and informally – what happens in its everyday practices.

The police occupational culture

Academics have argued that the police have a unique occupational culture. However, this culture is presented as overwhelmingly negative and is linked with rank-and-file officers. This culture is often associated with the perceived crime-fighting role of the police. The crime-fighting mission of policing, exaggerated by both police officers and researchers, has caused the worst characteristics of police behaviour to be attributed to police culture (Foster, 2003). These cultural features of policing have been the subject of numerous studies and are often referred to as the 'canteen culture' or 'cop culture'.

There has been a considerable body of research into the occupational culture of the police service (Chan, 2003; Fielding, 1988; Reiner, 1992, 2000; Skolnick, 1996; Waddington, 1999), which has identified the core elements as being a sense of mission, the desire for action and excitement, action-orientated behaviour and cynicism, featuring danger, solidarity, isolation, pragmatism, authority and an 'us and them' division of the social world. In addition, other features such as machismo, intolerance, prejudice and conservatism have been acknowledged.

It has been suggested that, as the police service has parallels to a military culture, in that it is a hierarchical and disciplined occupation that traditionally recruited from the blue-collar and working-class communities, it is associated with a form of masculinity that emphasises physical strength (Miller et al., 2003). The legacy of the military ethos is reflected in the cultural forms of uniform, rank and the ideological focus on exclusivity, masculinity, desire for action and an exalted view of violence. The band of brothers represented in the thin red line of soldiers defending the country is replaced in policing terms by what Reiner describes as the *thin blue line between anarchy and order* (1992, p112).

Characteristics of 'cop culture'

Mission, action, cynicism and pessimism

- **Mission** – Policing is perceived by the police as a mission, not just a job but a way of life. The police protect the weak and helpless against predatory villains and preserve a valued way of life. In doing so, the police regard policing as a game of wit and skill in the oppression of lawbreakers.

- **Action** – Policing is a positive world of action that is symbolised by the 'chase'. This chase is often referred to as 'twos and blues' and is viewed as a combative role in which the police protect 'good guys' from 'bad guys'.

- **Cynicism** – The police deal with very inhumane aspects of life. This leads them to develop a cynical interpretation of their immediate surroundings and the criminals they police.

- **Pessimism** – Linked to cynicism is pessimism, which typically places the police as a beleaguered minority.

Suspicion

Operational policing is characterised by the need to be alert for signs of trouble, danger and evidence/intelligence. Thus, the police have developed finely detailed cognitive maps of the social world so that they can readily predict and deal with the behaviour of others in different contexts without losing authority. This can result in suspicion and mistrust of certain social groups, resulting in stereotyping. The critical issue is not the existence of stereotyping, but the extent to which it is reality-based rather than being applied in a discriminatory and counterproductive manner.

Conservatism

Evidence has demonstrated that police officers are conservative, not necessarily just in the political meaning, but that they are more authoritarian and intolerant of liberal behaviour. They prefer crime control strategies where they can enforce the law and there is little room for non-conformity.

Machismo

The police world is permeated by machismo, which has become embedded in the recruitment and promotion processes. Policing was traditionally viewed as a 'job for the boys'. It has been argued that both excessive alcoholic and sexual indulgences of the police are a product of machismo.

Isolation and solidarity

The social isolation of the police has arisen from shift work, erratic hours, aspects of the discipline code, tension from the job, covert knowledge they have about the community and a general hostility from some members of the community. Solidarity is the product of isolation as well as of the nature of policing. Police rely on each other in dangerous situations. In addition, conflicts and divisions within the organisation lead to solidarity between departments and ranks.

This creates an 'us and them' outlook, where 'them' can either be other police departments or ranks, or community groups that need to be targeted and policed. These groups are exemplified by their worst characteristics and behaviours in order to define relationships with them. Seven key groups have been identified.

- **Good class villains** – professional or experienced criminals who are worth pursuing.

- **Police property** – typically those low-status and powerless groups that have at times been portrayed as distasteful or problematic. The prime function of the police is to control and segregate these groups to keep the streets safe. Legislation can effectively create new police property.

- **Rubbish** – people who make calls that are seen as messy, intractable, unworthy of attention or the complainant's own fault. Domestic violence was once regarded as rubbish.

- **Challengers** – people who routinely penetrate the secrecy of the police culture and challenge their decision making and control. These may include other agencies, the legal profession and the media.

- **Disarmers** – groups that receive specially sympathetic police treatment because of their vulnerability. They may include women, children and the elderly.

- **Do-gooders** – anti-police activists who challenge police authority and autonomy.

- **Politicians** – while they have the power to make the law, they are also viewed as not understanding the world of policing.

Racial prejudice

Arising from police conservatism comes racial prejudice, for example police suspicions and hostility towards minority groups. This can be illustrated vividly in numerous riots between the police and ethnic minority groups. The Scarman and Macpherson Reports both highlighted racial prejudice within policing.

Pragmatism

Police operations are about providing an immediate response to a crisis or perceived crisis. Therefore, a necessary pragmatism develops to deal with such circumstances. However, a by-product of pragmatism is a lack of innovation and experimentation within the craft of policing.

(Based on Reiner, 2000; adapted from Grieve et al., 2007, pp117–18)

REFLECTIVE TASK

Do you think that the police service attracts people that already demonstrate the characteristics of a cop culture, or that police officers are influenced by police culture once they have joined the service?

There are two broadly competing theories that explain police culture. One is that people who display these characteristics choose to join the police force because it is attractive to them as a career. The other theory is that these behaviours and attitudes are learned in the nature of police work and socialised through interaction with more 'seasoned' police officers (Chan, 1997; Waddington, 1999). Research has suggested that the attitude of new police recruits is a strong commitment to public service and they do not demonstrate any distinctive police personality. Indeed, their attitudes are no different from those in society.

However, although new recruits may initially have aspirations to serve the community, there is evidence that, within a short period of time, police officers begin to reassess these values towards one that is more focused on crime-fighting and what they perceive as being real police work. It has been asserted that the two-year police probationary period allows a process of socialisation for 'cop culture' to manifest itself at the individual level (Fielding, 1988).

Recent studies have exposed the heterogeneous nature of police culture and the significance of police officers being active agents in the formation, acceptance or rejection of particular aspects of it (Chan, 1996). Police culture often manifests itself in different forms both within and between forces. Informal rules and behaviour are embedded in specific practices and understandings according to situational and organisational circumstances. Police culture is also a reflection of the power structures that exist in policing communities; it provides an understanding of how police view the social world and how their role in it is crucial to the function of the police.

Learning the police culture

Despite the mundane and routine nature of police work, new recruits soon learn that policing can be difficult, stressful and demanding, often involving tasks that are emotionally challenging, unpredictable and traumatic. This can include dealing with sudden deaths, including suicides and fatal accidents, public disorder, child abuse, pub fights and domestic violence. Foster (2003) argues that these incidents have a powerful impact, which often remains unacknowledged, in shaping police officers' approach to their work. This is why police culture is so dominant and emphasises the danger and uncertain aspects of the job. New recruits soon *learn that to survive their work practically and emotionally requires them to be one of a team* (Foster, 2003, p202). They also become aware that other members of the team have the power to accept or reject their membership of that team. So the probationer period is as much about informal conversations and groupings as formal teaching and training. This process represents an important transition for the new recruit from 'autonomy' to 'solidarity', where the new officer moves from being an individual to being part of a group (Fielding, 1988).

The informal experiences of new recruits have an intense impact on police officers' attitudes and behaviour. Schein (1996) asserts that the transition from autonomy to solidarity represents a psychological contract that formalises the relationship between the recruit and the members of the group. This formalisation process defines the group's norms and practices as well as what is expected from members. Hunt and Manning (1991) illustrate this process in their study of police lying and how the nature of police work, and officers' responses to it, open up a moral and practical minefield that creates a backdrop for a range of illegitimate behaviour and abuse. Hunt and Manning argue that, in some cases, lying is seen as *good police work* and inspired by good intent, while in other cases it is viewed as *bad police work* (Foster 2003, p205).

Good lying could include police lying to victims' families to reduce the distress of an incident, whereas bad lying could be falsifying evidence. Although police lying can be seen as a continuum of good to bad, Foster (2003) argues that new recruits quickly begin to learn that the law is enforced inconsistently and differentially. This aspect of their role is reinforced by 'stories' reiterated by more experienced officers, who state that in order 'to get the job done' they need to engage in corner-cutting techniques through informal means rather than adhering to the rule of law. Learning to lie is therefore key to becoming a member of the group, and members expect their colleagues to collude in their lies. Hunt and Manning (1991) conclude that lying is so intrinsically embedded in the police officer's working practice that officers assume that this is the way the world works. However, Schein (1985) makes the point that cultures are a crucial part of an organisation's success and can represent a positive group learning process through the reinforcement of successful problems. The police, as an organisation, are confronted by situations to which an immediate response is required. This group learning process allows the police to develop a comprehensive knowledge of solutions that they are able to apply to incidents that demand immediate intervention. Therefore, Schein argues that there are aspects of the police culture that are of positive benefit to the police service.

PRACTICAL TASK

- *Can you give another example of 'good' lying and one of 'bad' lying?*

- *What moral and ethical considerations are involved when a police officer lies?*

- *Can there be any justification for a police officer to lie?*

- *How do police officers reconcile the guilt and remorse associated with lying?*

REFLECTIVE TASK

The police were called to the scene of a vehicle collision. One car had been stolen and the driver of that vehicle was a known prolific offender who was wanted on a warrant. The driver of the other vehicle had apprehended the criminal as he tried to run away from the scene and held him until the police arrived. The police officer noticed that the tax disc in the vehicle of the man who had apprehended the criminal was out of date.

- *Should the police officer issue a penalty notice to the driver for an out-of-date tax disc? Explain your answer.*

- *Are there any cases where it is appropriate to use discretion in enforcing, or not enforcing, the law?*

- *What would be the reasons for some police officers issuing a penalty notice in this case and for other officers not doing so?*

Police culture within and outside the police organisation

Although police culture can at one level develop vital trust relationships and team bonding required for occupations that respond to uncertain and dangerous situations, it can also allow groups of people to identify against other groups, leading to 'us and them' situations. This can occur both within and outside the organisation. Such situations can result in exclusionary and hostile behaviour, generating problems for other groups within society as well as other police colleagues. Cain (1973) undertook an in-depth study of police in Birmingham and Suffolk. This study found officers to be isolated and concerned only with their own police group activities and interests. This included the pursuit of criminals by whatever means were necessary (even illegal acts of violence and control). Emphasis was on loyalty to the group over all other loyalties that a police officer may have.

Smith and Gray (1985) studied the Metropolitan Police Service and found that informal norms were more significant than formal rules (for example, internal informal discipline by peers rather than external sanctions). The distinction was made by patrol officers between 'good' police work (for example, arresting criminals and excitement) and 'rubbish' police work (for example, domestic disputes and boring patrols). The research observed how police officers working in the Criminal Investigation Department (CID) were concerned with dominance and not losing face. Smith and Gray concluded that this form of mindset was strongly macho and was socialised through four particular elements.

- **Alcohol** – socialising together and consuming large amounts of alcohol was normal. Not drinking was seen as unprofessional and unmanly.

- **Violence** – the exercise of violence was synonymous with the exercise of authority.

- **Sex** – sexist language by the predominantly male officers led to the denigration of women.

- **Lack of sympathy** for others.

REFLECTIVE TASK

Loyalty is generally considered to be a good quality for a person to possess. Consider the ethical dilemmas in relation to police 'group loyalty' in the context of police officers working in a specialised police department such as covert investigations or child protection.

- *Are some police departments or tasks more susceptible to the development of group loyalty and therefore solidarity?*

- *Would a code of ethics for policing assist in the prevention of corruption in such departments?*

A typology of police officers

There has been research into how individual police officers respond to the same or similar situations. From this research academics have been able to produce a typology of police officers that helps explain why there may be different responses to similar incidents. Reiner (1978) identifies four different types of policing styles.

- **The Uniform Carrier** – this officer is lazy, disillusioned and cynical. Where possible, he or she will avoid any form of police action or activity. Reiner (2000) has argued that these officers are the result of career disappointment prior to a sense of mission, perhaps due to the overly bureaucratic policing process with excessive paperwork and little crime-fighting activity.

- **The New Centurion** – this officer believes that the role of the police is crime-fighting and maintaining the thin blue line between order and lawlessness. This type of officer is distrustful and is suspicious of the public, and perceives certain groups as police property that need to be dealt with using force and coercion.

- **The Professional** – the professional is a career-minded police officer who has a good knowledge of the police role and function. These officers are able to effectively develop finely honed policing skills to provide an effective service to the public.

- **The Bobby** – this officer is able to apply a range of policing techniques to situations that are effective and achieve the right outcomes. Such officers are knowledgeable about local issues and events that enable them to provide a balanced solution to problems.

REFLECTIVE TASK

- *How do you think each of the different types of police officer would deal with the issue in the reflective task about loyalty outlined above?*

- *Could any one outcome of the different police approaches above be considered more or less ethical than another?*

- *Can the typology of police officers above help to identify those officers who are more likely to act ethically and those who may act unethically?*

Waddington (1999) has cautioned about drawing conclusive links between theories of police culture and the behaviour and actions of police officers in the course of operational duty. He argues that police culture, or 'cop culture', is no more than 'stories and narratives' told within the 'canteen' or backstage locations that only tenuously link with operational reality. From his research he coined the term 'canteen culture' and found that officers on patrol were neither distinctly cynical nor authoritarian in their attitudes. This 'oral culture' was part of a broader coping strategy to help officers deal with a stressful occupation. He concluded that police officers were similar to social workers in their approach to responding to violent situations and emphasised that the police are a product of the society they serve.

REFLECTIVE TASK

There is some evidence that the police have systematically different beliefs about the criminality of men and women. Horn and Hollin (1997) took a sample of police officers and a broadly similar comparison group who were not police officers. A questionnaire was used to extract ideas about female and male offenders. The results revealed three dimensions of underlying beliefs and ideas about criminals.

- *Deviance – includes beliefs such as 'trying to rehabilitate offenders is a waste of time and money' and 'in general, offenders are just plain immoral'.*

- *Normality – this was reflected by agreeing with statements such as 'there are some offenders I would trust with my life' and 'I would like associating with some offenders'.*

- *Trust – this was measured by concerns such as 'I would never want one of my children dating an offender' and 'you have to be constantly on your guard with offenders'.*

Horn and Hollin presented two versions of the questionnaire – one with female offenders as the subject, the other with male offenders as the subject. Women offenders were seen as less fundamentally bad (deviant) than men who offend. This was true irrespective of the gender of the police officer. Compared with the non-police group, police officers saw offenders as fundamentally deviant or bad. The police viewed offenders as less normal than the general public, although they tended to see offending women as more normal and like the general public than male offenders. They also regarded offenders as less trustworthy than did the general public and male offenders were seen as less trustworthy than female offenders.

- *What can be concluded from the above research about police culture and police behaviour?*

- *Can the findings of the research explain how police officers may behave unethically towards male offenders?*

- *How can the research help inform an ethical and moral dimension in policing offenders?*

The final dimension to consider in this chapter is police officers' views on their own and other officers' misbehaviour and the impact this may have on police culture. In a study by Westmarland (2005) about the attitudes of police officers towards police corruption, unethical behaviour and minor infringement of police rules, the research revealed that officers viewed the various forms of misconduct differently according to how serious they thought the misconduct was. Certain misconduct, such as police officers stealing from a scene of crime, was viewed as more serious than behaviour involving illegal brutality against suspects and 'rule bending' in order to protect colleagues from criminal proceedings. The research also highlighted that police officers were only prepared to report their colleagues for misconduct if it related to acquisitive crime such as stealing from the crime scene. These findings support the existence of a 'blue code of silence' among police officers (Westmarland, 2005).

C H A P T E R   S U M M A R Y

The police possess a distinctive culture that is characterised by the beliefs, behaviour, thinking and interaction that police officers share in common. It refers to the combination of values, attitudes, prejudices and working practices found among police officers (Waddington, 2008). The wide of degree of discretion afforded to police officers can often act as *a cloak that hides stereotyping and prejudice* (Waddington and Wright, 2010, p53) and it is this aspect that has often been associated with the negative aspects of police culture. However, while police culture is more generally associated with negative behaviour, Schein has also argued that police culture can be an essential positive attribute in the police organisation. Ethical and valued policing practice can help negate the more negative aspects of dishonourable police practice and develop the positive aspects of police culture.

FURTHER READING

There are excellent books, chapters in books and journal articles relating to various aspects of what is generally termed police culture. However, Waddington's *Policing Citizens* (1999), Reiner's *The Politics of the Police* (2000) and Chan's *Changing Police Culture: Policing in a multicultural society* (1997) all provide excellent accounts.

REFERENCES

Cain, M (1973) *Society and the Policeman's Role*. London: Routledge and Kegan Paul.

Chan, J (1996) Changing Police Culture. *British Journal of Criminology*, 36: 109–34.

Chan, J (1997) *Changing Police Culture: Policing in a multicultural society*. Cambridge: Cambridge University Press.

Chan, J (2003) *Fair Cop: Learning the art of policing.* Toronto: University of Toronto Press.

Fielding, N (1988) *Joining Forces: Police training, socialization and occupational competence.* London: Routledge.

Foster, J (2003) 'Police Cultures', in Newburn, T (ed.) *The Handbook of Policing*. Cullompton: Willan Press.

Gregory, G and Lees, S (1999) *Policing Sexual Assault.* London: Routledge.

Grieve, J., Harfield, C and MacVean, A. (2007) *Policing: Sage Course Companion.* Sage

Horn, R and Hollin, CR (1997) 'Police Beliefs about Women who Offend'. *Legal and Criminological Psychology*, 2: 193–204.

Hunt, J and Manning, P (1991) 'The Social Context of Police Lying', *Symbolic Interaction*, 14(1): 1–20. Reproduced in Pegrebin, M (ed.) (2003) *Qualitative Approaches to Criminal Justice: Perspectives from the field.* Thousand Oaks, CA: Sage.

Miller, SL, Forest, KB and Jurik, NC (2003) Diversity in Blue: Lesbian and gay police officers in a masculine occupation. *Men and Masculinities*, 5(4): 355–85.

Morgan, D (1992) *Discovering Men.* London: Routledge.

Reiner, R (1978) *The Blue Coated Worker.* Cambridge: Cambridge University Press.

Reiner, R (1992) *The Politics of the Police.* Hemel Hempstead: Prentice Hall.

Reiner, R (2000) *The Politics of the Police*, 3rd edition. Oxford: Oxford University Press.

Schein, E (1985) *Organizational Culture and Leadership.* San Francisco, CA: Jossey-Bass.

Schein, E (1996) *Organizational Culture and Leadership*, 3rd edition. San Francisco, CA: Jossey-Bass.

Skolnick, J (1996) *Justice Without Trial.* New York: Wiley.

Smith, D and Gray, J (1985) *Police and People in London.* London: Gower.

Waddington, PAJ (1999) *Policing Citizens.* London: UCL Press.

Waddington, PAJ (2008) 'Police Culture', in Newburn, T and Neyroud, P (eds) *Dictionary of Policing.* Cullompton: Willan Press.

Waddington, PAJ and Wright, M (2010) *What is Policing?* Exeter: Learning Matters.

Westmarland,L (2005) Police Ethics and Integrity: Breaking the blue code of silence. *Policing and Society*, 15(2): 145–65.

USEFUL WEBSITES

www.acpo.police.uk – Association of Chief Police Officers

www.acpos.police.uk – Association of Chief Police Officers in Scotland

www.homeoffice.gov.uk – Home Office

www.justice.gov.uk – Ministry of Justice

www.skillsforjustice-nosfinder.com – Skills for Justice, National Occupational Standards

www.sqa.org.uk/sqa/33667.html – Scottish Qualifications Authority PDA Diploma in Police Service Leadership and Management: Professional ethics in policing

4 An ethical approach to equality and discrimination

CHAPTER OBJECTIVES

By the end of this chapter you should be able to:

- understand how police discrimination has negatively influenced the policing of ethnic minority communities;
- understand how this discrimination has informed and influenced how ethnic minority police officers are treated within the police service;
- understand the impact of both the Scarman Report and the Macpherson Inquiry into policing ethnic minority groups within a thinking and ethical framework;
- understand how discrimination operates in relation to gender inequality and how leadership can affect discriminatory practice;
- understand your own values and prejudices and how these can influence your policing approach;
- understand what is meant by institutional racism and individual racist behaviour.

LINKS TO STANDARDS

This chapter provides opportunities for links with the following Skills for Justice, National Occupational Standards (NOS) for Policing and Law Enforcement 2008.

AA1	Promote equality and value diversity.
AE1.1	Maintain and develop your own knowledge, skills and competence.
CA1	Use law enforcement actions in a fair and justified way.
HA1	Manage your own resources.
HA2	Manage your own resources and professional development.
HB11	Promote equality of opportunity and diversity in your area of responsibility.
POL1A1	Use police action in a fair and justified way.
POL1A2	Communicate effectively with members of communities.

With the introduction of the Qualification and Credit Framework (QCF), it is likely that the term 'National Occupational Standards' will change. At the time of writing it is not clear what the new title will be, although it is known that some organisations will use the term 'QCF assessment units'.

Links to current NOS are provided at the start of each chapter; however, it should be noted that these are currently subject to review and it is recommended that you visit the Skills for Justice website to check the currency of all the NOS provided: www.skillsforjustice-nosfinder.com.

Introduction

In Chapter 3 we explored how the police possess a distinctive culture within which they enforce the law and apply their moral judgements in doing do. Kleinig (1996) argues that, although the police are public servants, they are distant from the public they serve as the result of their law enforcement and public order maintenance roles. The law enforcement role epitomises how the public view the police and it is to a greater extent how the police perceive themselves. This has created the position where, *As law enforcers they are seen as monitors of human conduct, standing* over against *rather than* with *their client public* (Kleinig, 1996, p68).

As a consequence, the police can have limited social interaction and form fewer networks with members of their community. As we saw in Chapter 3, some of the features of police culture include prejudice on the basis of gender, sexuality and race, combined with a relatively isolated position in society. This chapter will explore the issues of equality and their relationship with ethics.

Policing and racism

Policing ethnic minorities and racism within the police organisation have long been concerns for academic commentators. Recently, BBC research has revealed that the first black police officer in England and Wales was PC John Kent, the son of a Caribbean slave, who joined the police force in Carlisle in 1837. In 1841, he gave evidence at the Carlisle Assizes in the case of a police constable being murdered by a blow to the head as an election crowd became uncontrollable in the city centre and overwhelmed the Chief Constable and about eight of his officers. Unfortunately, he was sacked after serving just seven years with Carlisle Constabulary for being drunk on duty – a common offence among police officers at that time (BHM, 2011).

However, there were no further records of black police officers until Norwell Roberts joined the Metropolitan Police Service in 1966. Roberts had a 30-year career with the police service, rising to the rank of detective. Two years later, Sislin Allen became Britain's first black policewoman:

> *On the selection day there were so many people there, the hall was filled with young men. There were ten women and I was the only Black person. On the day I joined I nearly broke a leg trying to run away from reporters. I realised then that I was a history maker. But I didn't set out to make history, I just wanted a change of direction.*
> (BHM, 2011)

While racist attitudes and thinking are prevalent in British society, research (Bowling and Phillips, 2002; Holdaway, 1997; Reiner, 2000; Smith and Gray, 1985) has demonstrated that racism and racial prejudice in police culture are more widespread and pervasive than in wider society. This included the findings that people from ethnic minority groups were perceived negatively and that racial prejudice and racist talk were *pervasive, expected, accepted and even fashionable* within the police service (Bowling and Phillips, 2003, p528).

Research has demonstrated that most people, including police officers, have a tendency to use stereotypes to classify people from different ethnic groups. Bowling and Phillips (2003) looked at a sample of police officers and found the behaviour listed in Table 4.1.

Table 4.1 Police stereotypes

Ethnic group	Police stereotype
Asians	Devious, liars, potential illegal immigrants
Black people	Engage in violent crime, drug abusers, incomprehensible, suspicious, hard to handle, aggressive, troublesome, tooled-up and lacking brainpower

Source: Bowling and Phillips (2003, p529)

REFLECTIVE TASK

- *How can racial prejudice impact upon police behaviour and responses to ethnic minority groups?*

- *How would such racial discrimination affect the behaviour of police officers towards their black and Asian colleagues?*

- *How would this make black and Asian colleagues feel about being police officers?*

- *Reflect on your own feelings and motivations about racial behaviour.*

Policing ethnic minority groups

The experience of ethnic minority groups being treated unfairly and discriminated against by the police can be found as early as the 1960s in a report by the West Indian Standing Council, which alleged that police engaged in a practice that was referred to as 'nigger hunting' (Hunte, 1966). There are records of police harassment and brutality continuing throughout the 1970s, including the policing of 'coloured immigrants'. The 1971 Immigration Act empowered the police and immigration authorities to detain and question people who they suspected of being illegal immigrants. A series of high-profile immigration raids was mounted during the early 1970s and this provided the context for systemic racial abuse of ethnic minority groups, particularly the black community, during this period. This form of racial profiling also occurred in the USA, where ethnic communities were targeted by law enforcement agencies.

The relationship between the police and black communities came to a head in 1980 in a series of violent riots that spread across the country. The St Pauls Riot in Bristol occurred when police raided the Black and White café, leading to the arrest of 130 people with 25 being taken to hospital, including 19 police officers. Sixteen of those arrested were prosecuted for riot but all were either acquitted, or had their charges dropped and were discharged after the jury failed to reach a verdict. The riot took place as a result of increasing racial tension, poor housing and alienation of young black males. At the time of the riot, the then Home Secretary William Whitelaw reported that the Chief Constable accepted that, although the police had made mistakes in policing the incident, there was little benefit in a public inquiry as it would only lead to the police being criticised unnecessarily (Dresser and Fleming, 2008).

Riots between black communities and the police then followed in other major cities and towns, including Brixton, Manchester, Liverpool and Birmingham. These riots, as the police and the black communities (mainly black youths) clashed in physical battles, were represented as the collapse of social order (Bowling and Phillips, 2003). Following these riots, Lord Scarman was appointed to chair a public inquiry.

The Scarman Report (1981) concluded that the riots were the result of anger and resentment of young black people against the police. Although he recorded that not all the rioters were black, he demonstrated that there was a significant problem in the policing of deprived inner-city areas with multicultural communities that were racially disadvantaged. The Scarman Report shifted from 'race relations' to 'community relations' as he identified the plight of ethnic communities in UK inner cities and their relationship with the rest of the community. Most notable was the conclusion that it was essential that all individuals were encouraged to secure a stake in their community and have a sense of responsibility for the area in which they live. The emphasis was not only that the community should have involvement in its local policing; greater importance was attached to community redevelopment and planning in order to counteract racial disadvantage. The Scarman Report did not directly apportion blame to the police but acknowledged that the *ill-considered, immature and racially prejudiced actions* (1981, p63) of some officers contributed to the riots. Following this, Lord Scarman's recommendations in relation to the police (Bowling and Phillips, 2003) were as follows.

- Identifying racial prejudice among police recruits.

- Recruiting more ethnic minority police officers.

- Improving community relations.

- Closer supervision of front-line police constables.

- Better management training for sergeants and inspectors.

- Making racial behaviour a dismissible offence.

- Greater public consultation to increase confidence in the police.

- Lay visitors for police stations.

- An independent element for complaints against the police.

However, despite the Scarman Report recommendations, problems continued and, in 1985, riots in Handsworth, Birmingham, resulted in the deaths of two Asian men, with more than 100 people injured. Later that year, the Broadwater Farm Riots occurred in London. PC Keith Blakelock was killed and more than 250 people were injured. In 2001, there was a short but intensive period of rioting in Bradford, West Yorkshire, which took place as the result of heightened tension between the ethnic minority communities and certain white groups. This tension had been fuelled by confrontation between far right groups such as the British National Party and the National Front. In July 2001, groups of between 30 and 100 white youths attacked police and Asian-owned businesses. Initially, there were 500 police dispersed to contain the riot, but later this increased to almost 1,000. What started as a riot turned into a race-related disturbance, with targeting of businesses and cars, along with numerous attacks on shops and property. More than 300 police officers were injured during these riots. However, thereafter riots between minority groups and police dwindled (Keith,1993).

Macpherson Report

While the Scarman Report argued that 'institutional racism' (a term used in the Macpherson Report), did not exist in the police service, it did acknowledge that some police officers exhibited racist behaviour towards ethnic minority groups. The acceptance that some police officers may be racist, and that this was reflected in their professional behaviour and actions, coincided with the official recognition of violent attacks on ethnic groups more generally. In 1981, the government and police started to record racist incidents and in the mid-1980s it was established as an urgent priority for the Home Office, the police and other statutory agencies (Bowling, 1998). However, it was to be the racist murder of Stephen Lawrence in 1993 that was to bring the issue to public attention.

CASE STUDY

Stephen Lawrence, a black British teenager, had spent the evening with his friend Duwayne Brooks on 22 April 1993. They were travelling home in London by a series of bus journeys. When Stephen and Duwayne reached Eltham, they were waiting at the bus stop when a group of young, violent, racist men crossed the road, surrounded Stephen and stabbed him twice, killing him. There were three witnesses waiting at the bus stop at the time of the attack. However, all three stated that the attack was quick and none was able to identify the suspects. A case was brought against two suspects, Neil Acourt (aged 17 years) and Luke Knight (aged 16 years) with the charge of murdering Stephen. However, this case was dropped on 29 July 1993 by the Crown Prosecution Service which stated that there was insufficient evidence.

In 1994, Mr and Mrs Lawrence took out a private prosecution against the two initial suspects and three others. However, the charges against the original two suspects were dropped before the trial due to lack of evidence and the three remaining suspects were acquitted at trial when the judge ruled that the evidence given by Duwayne Brooks was inadmissible. On 14 February 1997, the Daily Mail *newspaper published pictures of the five suspects believed to have killed Stephen and referred to them as 'murderers', challenging them to sue the paper for libel if they were wrong.*

In February 1999, police officers who were investigating the initial police investigation disclosed that the police had received three anonymous telephone calls from the same woman giving details of the suspects and the original detectives had not followed up on the action.

Following the 1997 General Election, Sir William Macpherson was commissioned by the then Home Secretary, Jack Straw, to undertake an inquiry into the death of Stephen Lawrence. The Macpherson Report (1999) concluded that the initial police actions at the scene of the murder were grossly inadequate and that the initial investigation was flawed by missed opportunities and the investigation was inadequate and incompetently conducted. The inquiry also revealed that the police were given names of the perpetrators within a few days of the murder from over 20 different sources, but the investigation team were either slow to follow up the information or failed to follow it up at all. The Macpherson Inquiry concluded:

> There is no doubt but that there were fundamental errors. The investigation was marred by a combination of professional incompetence, institutional racism and a failure of leadership by senior officers.

(1999, para. 46.1)

PRACTICAL TASK

Access the Macpherson Report online at www.archive.official-documents.co.uk/document/ cm42/4262/4262.htm.

- *What did Sir William Macpherson mean in his report by 'professional incompetence'?*

- *List five particular elements/areas of the police investigation that Sir William Macpherson referred to as being professionally incompetent.*

- *From your reading of the Macpherson Report, was the investigation flawed because of professional incompetence or institutional racism?*

- *How many recommendations did Sir William Macpherson make in his inquiry and how many of them related to or touched upon aspects of race and/or diversity?*

- *Consider Scarman's allegations of 'ill-considered, immature and racially prejudiced actions of some officers' in light of the findings from the Macpherson Report.*

While the Macpherson Report criticised the police for professional failure, it concluded that this alone was not the reason for police incompetence and suggested that it was because Stephen Lawrence was black that this led to police officers not being as competent as they should have been, particularly in relation to the initial investigation at the scene of the crime, the treatment of Mr and Mrs Lawrence and Duwayne Brooks, and the use of inappropriate and offensive language. The report claimed that the police service as an organisation was 'institutionally racist' and Macpherson defined this as:

> *The collective failure of an organisation to provide an appropriate and professional service to people because of their colour, culture, or ethnic origin. It can be seen or*

detected in processes, attitudes and behaviour which amount to discrimination through unwitting prejudice, ignorance, thoughtlessness and racist stereotyping which disadvantage minority ethnic people.

(Macpherson, 1999, para. 6.34)

The Macpherson Report also quotes Bowling (1998):

*Institutional racism is the **process** by which people from ethnic minorities are systematically discriminated against by a range of public and private bodies. If the result or **outcome** of established laws, customs or practices is racially discriminatory, then institutional racism can be said to have occurred. Although racism is rooted in widely shared attitudes, values and beliefs, discrimination can occur irrespective of the intent of the individuals who carry out the activities of the institution. Thus policing can be discriminatory without this being acknowledged or recognised, and in the face of official policies geared to removal of discrimination. However, some discrimination practices are the product of **uncritical** rather than unconscious racism. That is, practices with a racist outcome are not engaged in without the actor's knowledge; rather, the actor has failed to consider the consequences of his or her actions for people from ethnic minorities. Institutional racism affects the routine ways in which ethnic minorities are treated in their capacity as employees, witnesses, victims, suspects and members of the general public.*

(Quoted in Macpherson, 1999, para. 6.33)

REFLECTIVE TASK

Given the definitions of institutional racism above, consider the following.

- *What is the difference between an individual behaving in a racist way and institutional racism?*

- *Do you know anyone who has demonstrated racist behaviour or have you witnessed a racist incident?*

- *How did that make you feel?*

- *What would you do if a police colleague exhibited racist behaviour in front of you?*

- *What moral considerations does a police officer have to take into account in trying to engage with all sections of the community fairly?*

Racism and discrimination within the police service

If research and inquiries have highlighted discrimination against black and ethnic minority groups in the delivery of the police service, they have also shown that there is hostile treatment of ethnic minority police officers working within the police service. Increasing the number of ethnic minority officers was on the agenda of the Home Office prior to the 1981 Scarman Report (Bowling and Phillips, 2003). Research by the Home Office in 1999 concluded that the number of ethnic minority applicants to the police service was consistently lower than might be expected from their representation in the economically active population. The research also found that ethnic minority applicants were less likely than white applicants to be offered an interview, receive a formal offer of employment or be appointed on probation. Moreover, the retention figures for those ethnic minority applicants who succeeded in becoming police officers were lower than those of their white counterparts. Ethnic minority police officers were twice as likely as white officers to resign from the police service, and of more concern was that the dismissal rate of ethnic minority police officers was two to three times higher than for white officers.

Bowling and Phillips (2003) assert that, while ethnic minorities have traditionally found joining the police service more challenging than their white counterparts, once they have joined they faced considerable hostility from their colleagues:

> *Reading today Smith and Gray's (1985) study of 'the police in action', it is staggering to recall the language police officers used in speaking about black and Asian people. The centrality of racism in the subculture of the police served – and still does in some places – to alienate, marginalise and discriminate against ethnic minority officers.*
>
> (Bowling and Phillips, 2003, p541)

Neyroud and Beckley summarise the discrimination against ethnic minority police officers within the police service into four key areas of concern.

1. *The failure to recruit ethnic minority staff.*

2. *The poor record of retention and promotion for those who have been recruited.*

3. *The 'white' working culture of the organization.*

4. *Direct and indirect discrimination.*

(2001, p160)

From Neyroud and Beckley's four key issues of concern, consider the following.

REFLECTIVE TASK

Although there are many individual officers who are deeply committed to anti-racism within the police service, it is still criticised for 'collectively failing' minority ethnic police officers.

- *Using Neyroud and Beckley's four areas of concern above, how could active ethical leadership redress the issue of collective failure of the police organisation?*

Stop and search

The use of stop and search powers by the police has been one of the most controversial issues in policing ethnic minority communities, in both the UK and USA. The police have wide-ranging powers to stop and search individuals who they suspect have engaged, or are about to engage, in criminal activity and the power to stop and search is an investigative power used for the purpose of preventing and detecting crime in relation to a particular individual at a specific time. In 1984, the Police and Criminal Evidence Act (PACE) regulated the use of stop and search, stating that there had to be an objective basis for suspicion based on accurate and relevant facts, information and/or intelligence. However, it has been argued that, in practice, the police frequently use stop and search powers for other purposes, such as breaking up young groups of people on the street, for social control of groups who frequent specific areas at specific times and for gathering intelligence (Bowling and Phillips, 2003; Fitzgerald, 1999; Waddington et al., 2002). One of the most consistent findings of all the research on stop and search is that ethnic minority communities are far more likely to be stopped and searched by the police than white people. In 2007–08, there was a general increase in the use of stop and search powers, with over 1,035,438 stop and searches recorded in England and Wales. The main reason cited by officers was the suspicion of carrying drugs. The figures also showed that black people were still eight times more likely to be stopped and searched than white people (Home Office, 2009).

In trying to explain the disproportionality, academics have provided a number of different explanations. These include that some minority ethnic groups spend a greater proportion of their time on the streets and in other public places compared to their white counterparts (Fitzgerald, 1999; Waddington et al., 2002). However, as Lord Scarman noted: *some officers lapse into an unthinking assumption that all young black people are potential criminals* (1981, p64).

This type of stereotyping of ethnic minorities by police officers has been corroborated by a body of research, including a study undertaken by the Home Office, which identified that the disproportionality of stop and searches on ethnic minority groups was contributed to by police officers having a heightened suspicion of black people. The research further identified that this suspicion was deeply embedded and entrenched within the police organisation and, as such, had a corrosive impact upon community confidence in the police (Fiztgerald and Sibbitt, 1997).

REFLECTIVE TASK

You are on patrol with another police officer and you see a group of youths hanging around the bus shelter at the side of a park. It is 10.30 p.m. and dark and the youths are wearing hoodies with the hoods up. As you and your colleagues approach the group of youths, you see one of them put something into his mouth. Your colleague starts to speak with the youths, but they decline to engage in conversation and are not forthcoming about what they are doing.

- *What do you consider is the best course of action for you and your colleague to take?*

- *List the series of decisions you have made (consciously or subconsciously) in arriving at that action.*

- *Review the series of decisions you have made to see if you have made any discriminatory assumptions in arriving at your course of action.*

- *Ask your peers to review your decision-making process.*

- *After reviewing your decision-making process, would you still pursue your first course of action, or would you do something else?*

Gender and equality

Just as we have shown that there is discrimination and inequality in policing ethnic minority communities and that ethnic minority police officers are not treated as equally as their white counterparts, so too is there a history of female police officers being treated unfairly when compared to male police officers.

In 1981, women police officers accounted for only 8.6 per cent of the total police service for England and Wales, although this had risen to 13.2 per cent by 1993 and to 25 per cent by 2009. However, the figures are not equally distributed across the 43 different police forces and there are significant regional differences.

However, while acknowledging that there is still a long way to go before the gender gap is closed, the significant increase in female police officers in recent years has contributed towards a more fair and just role for female police officers than previously. In a study of the relationship between gender and police officers' perceptions of their job performance, Kaker (2002) found that both male and female officers perceived themselves as equally qualified to carry out tasks required in law enforcement, including the administrative and supervisory elements of the role. The research concluded that male and female police officers work equally well on their jobs and there are no significant differences in their job performance, capabilities and skills, even when the level of education and years of experience are controlled.

The Gender Agenda

In 1987, the British Association for Women in Policing (BAWP) was founded and was the only national organisation to embrace women of all ranks and grades. The main objective is to enhance the role and understanding of the specific needs of women who are employed by the police service. In 2000, BAWP was involved in the development of the Gender Agenda, which was a report to highlight the challenges of the working environment experienced by women officers in the police service. The aim of the Gender Agenda is to develop a common agenda in relation to the specific issues that affect women within the police service and to ensure they are supported in fulfilling their potential and aspirations. The Gender Agenda recognises the particular challenges faced by ethnic minority women and gay women and has five long-term aims.

- *For the police service to demonstrate consistently that it values women in policing.*

- *To achieve a gender, ethnicity and sexual orientation balance across the rank and grade structure and specialisms.*

- *To have a woman's voice in influential policy forums focusing on both internal and external service delivery.*

- *To develop an understanding of the competing demands in achieving a work/life balance and a successful career in policing.*

- *To have a working environment and equipment of the right quality and standards to enable women to do their job professionally.*

(www.bawp.org/assets/file/GA2%20Mark2.pdf)

BAWP is a proactive organisation that is constantly reviewing its role and aims. Therefore, there have been a number of updates to the Gender Agenda since its inception as it strives to make continuous progress for women in policing.

CASE STUDY

In 1983, Alison Halford became the first woman to reach the rank of Assistant Chief Constable in Merseyside and became widely known as the most senior female police officer in England and Wales. However, after nine attempts at further promotion she brought a successful sexual discrimination claim, which was supported by the Equal Opportunities Commission, against Merseyside Police Authority. Halford claimed to have faced sexual discrimination in her post as Assistant Chief Constable.

Her case documented the humiliation and criticism she had to endure in an attempt to force her to relent and end her case against the Police Authority. At her industrial tribunal, Halford was cross-examined for over two weeks in a case that was abandoned before her opponents were subjected to the same treatment. Although Halford was awarded a settlement, the justice of her case remained unchallenged, as did her integrity. Alison Halford's case revealed the extent of male domination in the police service and the inadequacy of both internal and external procedures to address gender-based grievances.

One of the issues in the case of Alison Halford was the use of unlawful covert surveillance conducted against her by her senior male colleagues. This resulted in a landmark ruling at the European Court of Human Rights about the need for legislation to allow telephone tapping in the UK.

REFLECTIVE TASK

Access the case, Halford v. UK (1997) 24, European Human Rights Report 523, and consider the following.

- *What are the ethical considerations of a police officer's right to privacy as an employee?*

- *What role has leadership to play in defining gender issues for the police service?*

C H A P T E R   S U M M A R Y

This chapter introduced not only how discrimination and prejudice can impact on policing ethnic minority groups, but also how it affects ethnic minority police officers within the police service. In particular, it examined the Scarman Report and the Macpherson Inquiry to understand how discrimination is conceptualised and understood within the broader context of policing. Using these reports, the chapter highlighted the differences between institutional racism and individual racist attitudes. It explored an understanding of your own values and prejudices and how these may influence, either wittingly or unwittingly, your police practice. The chapter examined how discrimination can manifest itself in gender inequality and how leadership can impact upon such practice. The role of leadership and individual reflection can make a contribution to anti-racist behaviour and practice at both the individual and organisational level.

FURTHER READING

Much of the reading in this chapter is drawn from a variety of chapters from a range of disciplines. However, Bowling and Phillips' *Racism, Crime and Justice* (2002) provides a comprehensive overview of policing ethnic minority communities in relation to ethnicity, inequality and racism. The first major study of policing and racism is Hall et al.'s *Policing the Crisis* (1978). The Home Office study, *Assessing the Impact of the Stephen Lawrence Inquiry* (Foster et al., 2005), also provides an update of how the recommendations of the Macpherson Report have been conceptualised and implemented.

REFERENCES

BHM (Black History Month) (2011) Uniformed Services. Online at www.blackhistorymonthuk.co.uk/uni/first_in_the_force.html (accessed 20 November 2011).

Bowling, B (1998) *Violent Racism: Victimisation, policing and social context.* Clarendon Studies in Criminology. Oxford: Oxford University Press.

Bowling, B and Phillips, C (2002) *Racism, Crime and Justice.* London: Longman (Pearson).

Bowling, B and Phillips, C (2003) Policing Ethnic Minority Communities, in Newburn, T (ed.) *Handbook of Policing.* Oxford: Oxford University Press.

Dresser, M and Fleming, P (2008) Bristol: Ethnic minorities and the city, 1000–2001. Chichester: Phillimore.

Fitzgerald, M (1999) *Searches in London under Section 1 of the Police and Criminal Evidence Act.* London: Metropolitan Police Service.

Fitzgerald, M and Sibbitt, R (1997) *Ethnic Monitoring in Police Forces: A beginning.* Home Office Research Study 173. London: Home Office.

Foster, J, Newburn, T and Souhami, A (2005) *Assessing the Impact of the Stephen Lawrence Inquiry.* Home Office Study HORS 294. London: Home Office.

Hall, S, Critcher, C, Jefferson, T, Clarke, J and Roberts, B (1978) *Policing the Crisis: Mugging, the state and law and order.* London: Palgrave Macmillan.

Holdaway, S (1997) Some Recent Approaches to the Study of Race in Criminological Research: Race as a social process. *British Journal of Criminology*, 37(3): 383–400.

Home Office (2009) *Crime in England and Wales 2007/08: A summary of the main findings.* London: HMSO.

Hunte, J (1966) *Nigger Hunting in England?* London: West Indian Standing Conference.

Kaker, S (2002) Gender and Police Officers' Perception of their Job Performance. *Criminal Justice Policy Review*, 13(3): 238–56.

Keith, M (1993) *Race, Riots and Policing: Lore and order in a multi-racist society*. London: UCL Press.

Kleinig, J (1996) *The Ethics of Policing.* Cambridge: Cambridge University Press.

Macpherson, W (1999) *The Stephen Lawrence Inquiry.* Report of an Inquiry by Sir William Macpherson of Cluny, Cm 4262–1. London: HMSO.

Neyroud, P and Beckley, A (2001) *Policing, Ethics and Human Rights.* Cullompton: Willan.

Reiner, R (2000) *The Politics of the Police*, 3rd edition. London: Harvester Wheatsheaf.

Scarman, Lord (1981) *A Report into the Brixton Disturbances of 11/12 April 1981.* London: Home Office.

Smith, D and Gray, J (1985) *Police and People in London*. London: Gower.

Waddington, PAJ, Stenson, K and Don, D (2002) *Disproportionality in Police Stop and Search in Reading and Slough*. Report for Thames Valley Police.

USEFUL WEBSITES

www.acpo.police.uk – Association of Chief Police Officers

www.acpos.police.uk – Association of Chief Police Officers in Scotland

www.bawp.org – British Association for Women in Policing

www.homeoffice.gov.uk – Home Office

www.justice.gov.uk – Ministry of Justice

www.skillsforjustice-nosfinder.com – Skills for Justice, National Occupational Standards

www.sqa.org.uk/sqa/33667.html – Scottish Qualifications Authority PDA Diploma in Police Service Leadership and Management: Professional ethics in policing

5 Ethical leadership and management in policing

Introduction

The influence of police leadership over individual officers, whether through performance and disciplinary measures or through general tone-setting, may be substantial.

(NRC, 2004, p283)

This very carefully considered statement by the National Research Council formed part of the judgement of a panel of experts convened by the Council – a US scientific organisation – about the state of knowledge on the importance of police leadership. *The chief*, they went on to say, *is the main architect of police officers' street behaviour* (p283).

They concluded that leadership in policing matters for achieving ethical policing, as did the way in which the people, resources and performance of policing are managed. Yet there has been only limited attention given to the study of police leadership or management (Neyroud, 2011a).

No systematic analysis [has been] offered concerning the ways in which police leadership is:

(a) *like all other manifestations of leadership;*

(b) *like some other types of leadership (e.g. public service);*

(c) *like no other form of leadership (in virtue of its specific tasks and functions).*

(Adlam, 2003, p40)

Police leaders, on whole, believe that police leadership is different and more like (c) (Heffernan, 2003), but Caless's survey of Chief Police Officers in England and Wales found little consensus on what constituted good police leadership (Caless, 2011).

Nevertheless, a literature review for the Neyroud *Review of Police Leadership and Training* (2011a) identified a number of studies that reinforced the NRC research. The review concluded that a more professional and consistent model of police leadership, incorporating a strong strand of ethics, was essential for future excellence in policing.

The emphasis on effective leadership and management highlight a number of key ethical questions.

- How can leadership set the tone and support ethical behaviour?

- What styles of leadership do you consider are most effective at this?

- If the effective styles are 'adaptive' to situations, how do police officers learn to choose the styles best fitted?

- Are the effective styles related to the priorities and approach to policing or are they independent of this?

This chapter examines leadership and management in policing and their impact on ethics.

Consider some examples that you have witnessed or read about of good leadership in policing.

- *Why did you categorise your examples as 'good leadership'?*

- *Do you consider the examples are particular to policing or are they just good leadership in any context?*

- *Think about how the qualities you identified can be developed in policing.*

Leadership and management

Leadership and management are not mutually exclusive terms. *Leadership is a process that is similar to management in many ways* (Northouse, 2010, p6). Both require influence, working with people and the accomplishment of goals, but, while leadership is more concerned with direction, alignment and motivation, management is more focused on planning, organising and controlling (Kotter, 1990). Leadership is *a process whereby an individual influences a group of individuals to achieve a common goal* (Northouse, 2010, p3).

Northouse breaks each of these components down, but stresses that the real heart of leadership is 'influence'. This is not simply a trait or characteristic of the leader but a continuous 'process'. Moreover, he argues that the process of influence by interaction between the leader and followers is a two-way one, in which leaders affect followers and followers leaders. By contrast, management can also involve organising systems, structures and resources as well as people. Influence in management can often, therefore, be an indirect result of the interaction of these with the people in the organisation, as in the management of performance.

However, as Kotter (1990) has emphasised, effective organisations need both leadership and management, and the best organisations are those where the process of leadership is harnessed to the discipline of management. The two are distinct but connected, or as Bennis and Nanus put it: *Managers are people who do things right and leaders are people who do the right thing* (1985, p221).

This definition alone emphasises how closely good management and good leadership align to ethics, which, as we have emphasised in Chapter 1, are concerned with doing the right things for the right reasons. As Bennis and Nanus (1985) suggest, good leadership and management are the key ways in which any organisation seeks to achieve an ethical approach.

Neither leadership nor management is, however, the exclusive preserve of the Chief Constable or Chief Executive. Indeed, a growing body of research on leadership, in particular, suggests that more attention needs to be paid to the collective leadership of the organisation, rather than just individual senior leaders (Neyroud, 2011b). This chimes with a number of reviews of police failures, such as the Stephen Lawrence Inquiry

(Macpherson, 1999), in which the Metropolitan Police Service was condemned not just for the individual failures of senior officers but also for the *collective failure of the organisation* (p321). Similarly, most of the reasons why law enforcement organisations fail, in O'Hara's (2005) analysis of police failures, are collective failures of leadership and management.

Consider the following case studies.

CASE STUDIES

Rodney King

Darryl Gates was the Chief of the Los Angeles Police Department at the time of the Rodney King beatings. King, an African-American, was stopped by LAPD officers and subjected to a violent assault by a number of officers that was captured on video and led to a violent community reaction and the worst riots in LA history. Gates was well known as an advocate of firm law enforcement and a police service independent from political influence. This approach found LAPD wanting, because the force was unresponsive to changes in society and its leadership was at all levels cut off from external scrutiny. Gates' own personal style served to reinforce a type of leadership that had deep roots in the organisation.

The Soham murders

In 2002, two schoolgirls, Holly Wells and Jessica Chapman, were murdered by a school caretaker, Ian Huntley, at Soham in Cambridgeshire. The circumstances of the murders – particularly the way that Huntley had been allowed employment despite having a record of sexual offences – led to a Public Inquiry headed by Sir Michael Bichard. Bichard's report severely criticised the Chief Constable of Humberside Police, David Westwood, for ordering the destruction of criminal records of child abusers. It also criticised the Chief Constable of Cambridgeshire Constabulary, Tom Lloyd, as his force had failed to contact Humberside Police during the vetting procedure. Lloyd was censured by HMIC for being slow to cut short a holiday after the investigation had become the largest in the force's history. HMIC also criticised a 'lack of grip' on the investigation. Bichard also criticised the police service and Home Office for not implementing a national system of information sharing.

REFLECTIVE TASK

- *How do the above case studies demonstrate the importance of leadership and management in policing?*

- *What lessons have they for police leaders?*

- *Are there any different lessons for police managers?*

- *How far were the failures the result of individual leaders and managers and how far were they 'collective' or institutional failures?*

Leadership in policing: history and styles of leadership

A number of studies of policing have demonstrated that there is a variety of leadership styles employed by police officers and that these are, at least in part, a response to the particular context of the police force concerned. In one of the most famous, James Q Wilson's (1968) study of eight departments in the USA, Wilson felt that he could identify three distinct conceptions of the role and mission of policing with associated differences in leadership approach.

- The 'watchman', who favoured order maintenance and high levels of discretion for the front line.

- The 'legalist', focused on enforcement and bureaucratic rectitude.

- The 'service' chief, who paid more attention to community involvement.

Wilson suggested that the styles reflected context and history, so that, for instance, a 'legalist' often seemed to follow corruption problems in a 'watchman' department. This was frequently because the 'watchman' style had a tendency to push the legal boundaries of enforcement, leading to abuses that then needed a different 'legalist' style to correct. In this sense, the leadership style and mission of departments was an adaptive response to circumstances as much as a leadership choice for the chiefs, who were often selected because of the style that they espoused or the style that was exhibited by the department from which they came. Wilson's study emphasised how far leadership in policing has tended to be identified with the person of the Chief Constable.

Reiner (1991) described a somewhat similar distinction in styles in his study of Chief Constables. He suggested that a Chief Constable's leadership style was affected by four 'Ps': Period or fashion; Problems that they confronted; the Place they police; and their own Pedigree, including education, forces served in, and departments and offices occupied. He typified the Chief Constables that he interviewed as falling into one of four categories:

- **baron**: paternalistic, traditionalist and hierarchical;

- **bobby**: the bobby on the beat promoted to Chief Constable, relying on personal power;

- **boss**: controlling through authority not power;

- **bureaucrat**: more managerial and less reliant on personal power.

When Caless (2011) asked his Chief Officer respondents which of these they identified with, a majority stated that they adopted a 'mix of styles' and a substantial minority rejected the typology altogether.

Unsurprisingly, therefore, there has been a continuing debate about 'best fit' styles and about the applicability of different theories of leadership to the police service and of the differences between leadership and management (Mitchell and Casey, 2007). The dominant debate has tended to be one between the relative merits of transactional approaches as against transformational ones. Burns' (1978) contrast of leadership based on exchange (transactional) as against leadership through motivation and morality (transformational) is highly relevant to the issue of ethics.

Transformational versus transactional leadership

Transformational versus transactional leadership

Transformational   **Transactional**
Idealised influence   Contingent reward
Inspirational motivation   Constructive transactions
Intellectual stimulation   Management by exception
Individual stimulation   Active and passive
                                   Corrective transactions
                           (Adapted from Northouse, 2010)

Transformational leadership, as the box shows, centres on the processes whereby leaders are able to inspire followers to achieve great things – going the extra mile. It places a great emphasis on the leader both role modelling behaviours and articulating a clear vision for the organisation. Leaders need to listen and adapt to the needs and aspirations of their followers, who are motivated to follow and perform by the vision and the trust built by the interactions. By contrast, transactional leadership is more narrowly concerned with the nature and quality of the interactions – reward and correction – between the leader and followers. Motivation is connected to self-interest, and reward and punishment.

Transformational leadership has many strengths and a strong emphasis on values, but its requirement for the leader to set the vision and direction for the organisation has been criticised as placing too much emphasis on the 'heroic leadership' model and the individual role in leadership (Etter, 2009). It also tends to focus attention on leadership at the top of the organisation, devaluing the importance of front-line leadership, which tends to be more transactional in character.

In contrast, leadership development approaches in both the UK and Australia over the last two decades have sought to try to bring together a number of different theories and match them to changing challenges (Mitchell and Casey, 2007). The recognition that effective policing requires partnership and thus leadership beyond the authority of the organisation itself, the shift in gender roles and the recognition of the importance of collective leadership from front-line to strategic have all impacted on the national development models. As Mitchell and Casey set out, these models have sought to incorporate and present within a single approach trait, behaviourist and situational and contingency theories.

Nevertheless, given that the main concern of governments has been to encourage the police to respond to high levels of change in the organisation and its environment, there has been a trend to encourage a more transformational approach. This shift was explicitly encouraged by the government in the UK (Home Office, 2003), supported by research into the preferred leadership behaviours of police officers, which were *found to match closely with a style of leadership known as transformational* (Dobby et al., 2004, pv). As a result, the Home Office pushed hard for transformational leadership to be the preferred style.

This produced a significant dilemma for police leaders because, at the same time, the government also created a fundamentally transactional framework of accountability, incorporating contingent reward – financial bonuses based on target achievement – and management by exception through intervention in poorly performing forces by the HMIC and Police Standards Unit within the Home Office (Neyroud, 2006). Furthermore, the transformational aspirations of Chief Officers and senior officers were widely perceived by the front line and public to be compromised by the lure of significant transactional bonus rewards, encouraging them to meet centrally set targets (Loveday, 2008). This helped to illustrate one key aspect of transformational leadership that its proponents have argued is crucial to its success – trust between the leaders and followers.

It was clear from responses to the survey supporting the Neyroud Review (2011a) and Caless's survey of Chief Officers (2011) that there was some considerable confusion among police leaders as to what was the best approach to adopt. The answer might well be that the search for a single preferred style is a fool's errand. Haberfeld (2005) and Mitchell and Casey (2007) both argue that police leaders need a more adaptive approach and a broader-based leadership model. We are going to seek to explore that argument below with two case studies – Community policing and 'Compstat' policing – which represent two dominant approaches to policing over the past 25 years.

Two case studies: community policing and 'Compstat' policing

Community policing and 'Compstat' policing have both been developed over the past 30 years. They have become two of the dominant expressed philosophies of, respectively, local policing delivery and police management of crime. Indeed, most Chief Officers would probably avow that they are committed to one or both approaches. They emerged out of an era at the turn of the 1980s, where the older 'professional model' of policing, based around emergency response, volume crime investigation and patrol strategies, had been demonstrated to be of limited effectiveness (NRC, 2004).

Community policing places a strong emphasis on problem solving and community involvement, underpinned by an acceptance that the police alone could not tackle crime successfully. In contrast, Compstat policing starts with the presumption that police are central to controlling crime and can be more effective by better deployment and use of information. There is, therefore, an underlying tension between the two. Compstat presents a police-centric view of the world and places senior leaders at the centre of it, while community policing envisages the police as facilitators of change at a local level. The differences were recognised by a recent study (Willis et al., 2010) that sought to explore ways in which they could be better integrated. However, the two have very distinct implications for the mission of the organisation, and the style and approach to leadership.

Community policing has, arguably, been a policing philosophy since 1829. 'Peel's principles' placed a strong emphasis on prevention rather than detection. In the 1980s, a key addition to the older tradition was the discipline of 'problem-oriented policing' (POP). POP started from a clear and deliberately articulated rejection of the 'professional model' of policing, which Goldstein (1990), POP's intellectual architect, described as having made policing insular and reactive, leaving insufficient time and energy to focus on the problems that mattered most to the community.

Goldstein recognised that his approach required a revolution in thinking in the service. Rather than responding to calls for service, the police needed to understand the underlying problems, identify partners to assist them in solving them, engage the community in the process and, above all, focus on broader societal outcomes. At its heart, because one reason for its adoption was the acceptance that police could not control crime on their own, was a different conception of the police role in society. Thus, the police became a catalyst for action on crime rather than the monopoly provider.

Studies of problem-oriented approaches have demonstrated that Goldstein's approach is potentially significantly more effective than methods without it (Taylor et al., 2011). In Taylor et al.'s Jacksonville experiment (see p144), police approaches to tackling crime by standard response policing were compared to two alternatives: using targeted patrols in high-crime hotspots; and using problem solving in the hotspots. The researchers found that problem solving produced a substantially increased and more sustainable level of crime reduction.

Despite increasing evidence of effectiveness, community policing and POP have proved a real leadership challenge to implement. First, they rely on the identification of problems and engagement with the community by community-based patrol officers, who must, necessarily, become central to the organisation rather than rely on the more traditional response and detective officers. This radical change of priority and importance in the organisation has proved stubbornly difficult to implement.

Second, Goldstein suggested that a problem-oriented organisation needed to be leaner, with fewer layers and a different relationship between front-line officers, who were going to become the 'General Practitioners' of policing, and the specialists, managers and leadership of the organisation. He argued that *the concept [of POP] has implications for every aspect of management*. Above all, there needed to be changes in the approach to leadership that were *far more radical than anything that has been advocated in the past* (p152).

Goldstein encouraged the new police leader to focus on three things:

- articulating their values and the values that must permeate the organisation;
- demonstrating a strong commitment to problem solving (as it were the values in action);
- making *fundamental changes in the most common type of relationship that exists between leadership and the rank and file in a police agency* (p152).

There is a very clear overlay between Goldstein's proposed approach and the transformational leadership principles set out above. Yet it is equally true that community policing also relies on good-quality transactional management – good-quality supportive supervision, training and performance appraisal – that Goldstein argued had not been typical of police chiefs' 'administrative management', which had been more focused on keeping the 'professional' force out of trouble. The Neyroud Review (2011a) suggested that Goldstein's arguments were still highly relevant.

In some ways, the leadership challenges of Compstat appear more straightforward. Indeed, Weisburd et al. (2006) have suggested that Compstat is largely a better, more technological way of doing what police bureaucracies had always done. The system uses a combination of technology (better crime information linked to geographical mapping), devolved accountability for operational tactics to local commanders and a ruthless follow-up from the Chief Officer's team. According to one of its main architects, Jack Maple, the Assistant Commissioner of Crime in New York, it has four key principles.

- *Accurate, timely intelligence.*
- *Rapid deployment.*
- *Effective tactics.*
- *Relentless follow-up.*

(Maple, 2000, p32)

It is easy to see this approach simply as an exercise in tight operational management, because the overt focus is on planning, organising, deployment and control of resources. However, as Bratton makes clear in his own description of the approach (Bratton and Malinowski, 2008), the leadership component lies in the strong vision about the aim of crime control and the devolved authority accorded to local commanders. Bratton argued that a major part of his contribution to the 'turn-around' in New York lay in the overall vision of reducing crime, the strategies that were introduced to turn that vision into action and the focus on crime reduction that the Compstat process enforced.

The techniques that Bratton pioneered in New York have been immensely influential across policing in many countries. Compstat as a mechanism and philosophy for driving focus and direction in the police organisation has become as dominant as community policing. However, it has been accompanied by a running debate about the nature of the relationships between the Chief Officer and the local commanders. In Bratton's New York the wastage rate of commanders was high. Bratton argued that this was because many of those he inherited were incompetent. Either way, the New York style of Compstat could be seen as fundamentally transactional, dominated by reward and punishment, particularly for the local commanders.

In the UK, the context was very different and Compstat arrived in the midst of a central government drive to improve police performance (Loveday, 2008). However, its implementation in the UK quickly demonstrated some of the ethical dilemmas that can arise with a Compstat approach. Over the decade from 1997 to 2007, national government demanded more and more detailed performance targets. They also insisted that the main yardstick of success for senior officers was the achievement of the targets. As a result, there was more and more emphasis in the selection processes for senior leadership on the success on driving up performance. The behaviours that were being rewarded were tight transactional management of the performance figures, rather than engagement with the public or involvement of the workforce. It was argued in an independent review that this was taking the priorities of policing away from the very public that the police served (Flanagan, 2008). The result was a progressive abandonment of the nationally driven Compstat-style approach by first Labour and then the Coalition government.

REFLECTIVE TASK

A Home Secretary announces that the sole target for the police is 'fighting crime'. With reference to the discussion above about community policing and Compstat, consider the following.

- *What implications might this target have for the leadership approach and styles of the force?*

- *How would leaders following the two approaches differ in the way that they tackled the priority?*

The Compstat and community policing case studies are an important illustration of the leadership and management challenges facing policing. The reality is that those governing policing, both nationally and locally, are likely to want both approaches most of the time. Community policing is a very attractive approach for local policing and, underpinned by POP, has an increasing body of evidence to support it. Compstat policing provides a more overt emphasis on the police role in crime control and a strong thread of accountability for performance that is appealing to politicians at all levels. Yet, as we have seen, the leadership styles that they encourage are different: community policing seems more consistent with a transformational style; Compstat policing has a fundamentally transactional core.

Conclusion: a leadership model for policing?

The studies examined in this chapter – Wilson (1968), Reiner (1991), Mitchell and Casey (2007) and, most recently, Neyroud (2011a, b) and Caless (2011) – have all suggested that police leadership and management are affected by and should be adapted to context and challenges. The examination of the case studies of community policing and Compstat policing suggested that police leaders are likely to be required to lead in potentially contradictory ways. This begs the question as to whether it is possible to develop a consistent leadership model for policing.

Logically, the aim of such a model would be to support those leading policing with the best possible fit of leadership approaches matched to the unique nature of policing. The Neyroud Review (2011a) argued that it is certainly possible to outline the main features and, indeed, that such a model was essential as the basis for any long-term development approach for the collective leadership of the profession of policing.

The Neyroud Review concluded that the leadership model for policing needed to have a strong focus on four dimensions with a framework of a new emphasis on 'evidence-based professionalism'. The latter was argued to be important to support police leaders making the 'right decisions' based on the best evidence available and being able to ensure that their strategies produce operational and community benefits without unforeseen or unacceptable backfire. Just as the Hippocratic Oath demands that medical practitioners 'do no harm' to their patients while treating them, so a police practitioner must, as objectively and scientifically as possible, weigh the benefits of different policing approaches with the potential harms caused by them directly or indirectly. This new, more scientific approach was also advocated in Weisburd and Neyroud (2010).

The Neyroud Review then suggested that the key elements of the leadership model were as follows.

- **Ethics**: particularly because of the strong links that the review's research identified between the leadership approach and front-line behaviour.

- **Command**: a distinctive element of police leadership is the need to command and coordinate other resources of public services or civil society.

- **Accountability**: providing police managers and leaders at all levels with a clearer concept of their accountability and the relationship between their operational decisions and external oversight.

- **Business skills**: police managers have the stewardship of large publicly funded organisations and need the best skills to ensure the most efficient and effective use of those resources.

The review did not, as earlier Home Office reports (2003), prescribe a particular leadership style. Given what we have said above about the context and challenges of policing, this is not surprising. However, Neyroud (2011b) has argued that the renewed emphasis on direct democratic control over the police suggests a need to consider the approach, which has been described as 'authentic leadership' in preference to transformational styles.

Authentic leadership describes a leadership approach that is still in the early stages of development, but that Northouse states is *transparent, morally grounded and responsive to people's needs and values* (p237). It was developed in response to criticism of transformational leadership's perceived problems, such as an overemphasis on heroic leadership. It also reflects research such as Porter's study of Chief Executives, in which he demonstrated that humility, subordination of self to organisational and societal goals, and strong and consistent personal values were key to the legitimacy and success of CEOs (Porter and Nohria, 2010). Authentic leadership can be seen as a reaction to the type of overconfident, self-focused leadership that was perceived as leading to the 2008 financial crash and subsequent depression.

For police services such as that in England and Wales, which have entered a new era of political involvement in policing through the Police Reform and Social Responsibility Act 2011 and the introduction of directly elected Police and Crime Commissioners (PCCs), authentic leadership may offer significant advantages over the previously favoured transformational approach. The PCCs seem likely to assume the responsibility for the strategy, vision and priorities for policing as a result of their direct democratic mandate. In this context, which is very familiar to police leaders in most democratic countries, police leaders need to find a leadership approach that translates the political vision into operational reality, while not compromising ethical and professional standards to short-term political whim.

C H A P T E R   S U M M A R Y

In this chapter, we have explored the nature of leadership and, in particular, leadership in policing. We have discussed the relationship between leadership and ethical behaviour by police officers. We have demonstrated the way in which different policing styles affect the leadership approach best fitted and how this, in turn, affects the way that the police go about tackling their priorities.

FURTHER READING

There is an extensive literature on leadership, but a good introduction and summary is to be found in *Leadership: Theory and practice* by Northouse (2010). *The Review of Police Leadership* by Neyroud (2011) has an appendix that summarises the results of a systematic review of the existing evidence on effective police leadership. Caless's study of ACPO, *Policing at the Top* (2011), provides an excellent account of senior police leaders' views at a time of change.

REFERENCES

Adlam, R (2003) Nice People, Big Questions, Heritage Concepts, in Adlam, R and Villiers, P (eds) *Police Leadership in the 21st Century: Philosophy, doctrine and developments.* Winchester: Waterside Press.

Bennis, WG and Nanus, B (1985) *Leaders: The strategies for taking charge.* New York: Harper Row.

Bratton, WJ and Malinowski, SW (2008) Police Performance Management in Practice: Taking COMPSTAT to the next level. *Policing: A Journal of Policy and Practice*, 2(3): 259–66.

Burns, JM (1978) *Leadership.* New York: Harper Row.

Caless, B (2011) *Policing at the Top: The roles, values and attitudes of chief police officers.* Bristol: Policy Press.

Dobby, J, Anscombe, J and Tuffin, R (2004) *Police Leadership: Expectations and impact.* London: Home Office.

Etter, B (2009) The Masterchef Phenomenon: A new style of leadership for policing. Paper for the 6th Australasian Council of Women Policing (ACWAP) conference, Perth.

Flanagan, Sir R (2008) *A Review of Policing.* London: Home Office.

Goldstein, H (1990) *Problem-oriented Policing.* New York: McGraw-Hill.

Haberfeld, M (2005) *Police Leadership.* New York: Prentice Hall.

Heffernan, W (2003) Three Types of Leadership, in Adlam, R and Villiers, P (eds) *Police Leadership in the 21st Century: Philosophy, doctrine and developments.* Winchester: Waterside Press.

Home Office (2003) *Getting the Best Leaders to Take On the Most Demanding Challenges.* London: Home Office.

Kotter, P (1990) *A Force for Change: How leadership differs from management*. New York: Free Press.

Loveday, B (2008) Performance Management and the Decline of Leadership within the Public Services in the United Kingdom. *Policing*, 2(1): 120–31.

Macpherson, Sir W (1999) *The Stephen Lawrence Inquiry*. London: The Stationery Office.

Maple, J (2000) *The Crime Fighter*. New York: Broadway Books.

Mitchell, M and Casey, J (eds) (2007) *Police Leadership and Management*. Sydney: Federation Press.

Neyroud, P (2006) Ethics in Policing: Performance and the personalisation of accountability in British policing and criminal justice. *Legal Ethics*, 9(1): 16–35.

Neyroud, P (2011a) *Review of Police Leadership and Training*. London: Home Office.

Neyroud, P (2011b) Leading Policing in the 21st Century: Leadership, democracy, deficits and the new professionalism. *Public Money and Management*, 31(5): 347–55.

Northouse, PG (2010) *Leadership: Theory and Practice*. Thousand Oaks, CA: Sage.

NRC (National Research Council) (2004) *Fairness and Effectiveness in Policing*. Washington, DC: National Academies Press.

O'Hara, P (2005) *Why Law Enforcement Organisations Fail*. Durham, NC: Carolina Academic Press.

Porter, M and Nohria, N (2010) What is Leadership? The CEO's role in large, complex organisations, in Nohria, N and Khurana, R (eds) *Handbook of Leadership Theory and Practice*. Boston, MA: Harvard Business Press.

Reiner, R (1991) *Chief Constables*. Oxford: Oxford University Press.

Taylor, B, Koper, C and Woods, D (2011) A Randomized Controlled Trial of Different Policing Strategies at Hot Spots of Violent Crime. *Journal of Experimental Criminology*, 7: 149–81.

Weisburd, D and Neyroud, P (2010) *Police Science: Towards a new paradigm*. Washington, DC: National Institute of Justice.

Weisburd, D, Mastrofski, S, Willis, JJ and Greenspan, R (2006) Changing Everything So That Everything Can Remain the Same: Compstat and American policing, in Weisburd, D and Braga, AA (eds) *Police Innovations: Contrasting perspectives*. Cambridge: Cambridge University Press.

Wilson, JQ (1968) *Varieties of Police Behaviour: The management of law and order in eight communities*. Cambridge, MA: Harvard University Press.

Willis, JJ, Mastrofski, S and Kochel, TR (2010) Recommendations for Integrating Compstat and Community Policing. *Policing: A Journal of Policy and Practice*, 4(2): 182–94.

USEFUL WEBSITES

www.npia.police.uk – National Policing Improvement Agency

6 Ethical and moral considerations in the use of force

CHAPTER OBJECTIVES

By the end of this chapter you should be able to:

- recognise how ethics and morals are considered in the deployment of force;
- understand how legislation relating to the use of force provides ethical guidelines;
- identify the ethical theories that are appropriate in considering the legitimate use of force;
- describe the coercive powers and legitimate force that the police are empowered to use;
- understand the specific ethical issues in the use of lethal force.

LINKS TO STANDARDS

This chapter provides opportunities for links with the following Skills for Justice, National Occupational Standards (NOS) for Policing and Law Enforcement 2008.

AE1.1	Maintain and develop your own knowledge, skills and competence.
CA1	Use law enforcement actions in a fair and justified way.
HA1	Manage your own resources.
HA2	Manage your own resources and professional development.
POL1A1	Use police action in a fair and justified way.

With the introduction of the Qualification and Credit Framework (QCF), it is likely that the term 'National Occupational Standards' will change. At the time of writing it is not clear what the new title will be, although it is known that some organisations will use the term 'QCF assessment units'.

Links to current NOS are provided at the start of each chapter; however, it should be noted that these are currently subject to review and it is recommended that you visit the Skills for Justice website to check the currency of all the NOS provided: www.skillsforjustice-nosfinder.com.

Introduction

Following the formation of the Metropolitan Police Force in 1829, police officers were issued with truncheons and rattles as part of their uniform. The truncheon, a weapon of force, was to be used by police officers to maintain order and keep the peace, and the rattle was to be used to alert other police officers or members of the public to an incident. Therefore, at the inception of the police service it was assumed that police work could be dangerous and that use of force was a core element of policing (Bittner, 1991).

The use of force has been a contentious issue throughout the history of policing. The first police officer to die on duty in June 1830 was PC Joseph Grantham, who, after trying to stop a fight between two drunken men near King's Cross, was kicked to death. The jury concluded at his inquest that the verdict was 'justifiable homicide', as PC Grantham had caused his own death by *over-exertion in the discharge of his duty* (Explained.At, 2011). Therefore, it was considered that PC Grantham had used too much force in the context of the situation, so his death by the hands of the two drunken men was justified. Despite this verdict, British policing is synonymous with the use of legal force and, as Manning (1977) has argued, has legal authorisation for the use of lethal force. However, while the police may have greater legal powers than ordinary members of the public, they do not have the monopoly on the use of force; anyone can legitimately use force in certain circumstances, such as in self-defence.

However, many academics argue that use of force is a core feature of policing and that, although there is much talk about policing as a profession, much of its training is focused around the tenet that coercive power is a central feature of police life (Skolnick and Fyfe, 1993). However, McLaughlin (1992) asserts that, while police officers are authorised to use force to carry out their role, in reality they do not deploy force as often as the public perceive them do to so. Sherman (1982) also states that use of force is embodied within criminal justice, just as the monopoly on the legitimate use of force is the essence of the nation-state.

Research conducted in America showed in what circumstances force was used by police officers for the year 1999–2000 (see Table 6.1).

Table 6.1 Percentage of officer use of force by circumstance of encounter 1999–2000 (USA)

Type of incident in which force was used	Percentage
Disturbance	21
Domestic incident	11
Traffic stop	14
Investigation	6
Arrest	39

Source: IACP (2001, piii).

Kleinig maintains that, although the police are authorised to use force, the use of force must be limited in order that it may be controlled and regulated:

Generally, some form of social contract argument has been advanced to limit that authority to police. For, once we recognize that humans do not always accord to each other the respect that is appropriately owed to them, those whose rights are violated or threatened with violation are frequently not in the position to protect their rights.

(Kleinig, 1996, p98)

For Kleinig, it is therefore better to invest such authority in an agent of the state such as the police than retain it as an individual right. Although use of force is part of the social contract and authority has been given to the police to legitimately use force on behalf of the state, that authority has constraints in how and when force is deployed (Kleinig, 1996). In defining a basis of what restraints need to be considered for the acceptable use of force, conversely there must also be consideration as to when use of force is acceptable, and if it is acceptable how much force is considered reasonable.

This chapter is concerned with the ethical and moral considerations when the police use force. Kleinig (1996) argues that the very fact the police are authorised to use force presents a problem, not just because they can use force, but because any use of force against any other person is problematic. Therefore, Kleinig asserts that the use of force needs to be justified *both generally and specifically* (1996, p97).

Definitions of force

There is no agreed definition of what constitutes force as used by the police. Terrill defines police force as:

acts that threaten or inflict physical harm on citizens, or which could be measured according to the severity of harm it imposes on a citizen from least to most harmful.

(2001, p2)

The International Association of Chiefs of Police (IACP), in its study *Police Use of Force in America 2001*, defined police use of force as: *The amount of effort required by police to compel compliance by an unwilling subject* (2001, p1). More generally, force is defined by the *Oxford English Dictionary* as *the use of physical power or violence to compel or restrain*. So, in its broadest sense, the definition of force is the use of physical power or violence, with or without the use of weaponry, to compel or restrain a person in order to prevent harm or further harm to citizens.

If such a broad definition of the police use of force is accepted, it must also be accepted that how force is applied, the context in which it is applied and the amount of force deployed become critical factors if the police are to maintain their legitimate authority. Therefore, the laws that sanction the use of police force are imperative because, by default, they also help define it by how and when it is or is not legitimately deployed.

Legislation on police use of force

There are a number of pieces of legislation that govern the police use of force. Police officers are subject to the same rules as ordinary citizens but must meet higher standards than the public for two reasons. First, because police officers are authorised on behalf of the state to use force and are therefore trained to deploy force; they have to use approved methods of restraint and apply it reasonably, proportionately and legitimately, and it must be necessary to use it. Second, because the police service is a public body, officers have an obligation under the Human Rights Act 1998 (HRA) not to use force that may be considered inhumane and/or degrading.

Therefore, the benchmark as to whether police use of force is lawful is whether it complies with the HRA and whether it was reasonable, proportionate, legitimate and necessary.

In England and Wales, the use of reasonable force is provided for under section 3 of the Criminal Law Act 1967. This encompasses both the police and any other person and states:

A person may use such force as is reasonable in the circumstances in the prevention of crime, or in effecting or assisting in the lawful arrest of offenders or suspected offenders or persons unlawfully at large.

In addition, section 117 of the Police and Criminal Evidence Act 1984 confers the power on constables to use reasonable force provided it is proportionate, lawful, appropriate and necessary.

Further provision in relation to when force is 'reasonable' is set out in section 76 of the Criminal Justice and Immigration Act 2008. The Act clarifies issues relating to the common law defence of self-defence and the use of reasonable force insofar as not to commit an offence under the Criminal Law Act 1967. The Act considers whether the person using force was entitled to rely on self-defence and whether the degree of force used was reasonable in the circumstances.

Finally, when determining whether the use of force was lawful in any particular situation, articles 2, 3 and 8 of the HRA are considered. These are the rights that are most likely to impact on the use of force:

- **Article 2: The right to life**

  This states that everyone's right to life shall be protected by law and that loss of life is only lawful if it results from the use of force, provided that no more force is used than absolutely necessary and only in the following circumstances: in defence against persons using unlawful violence; in order to make a lawful arrest or prevent the escape of a person lawfully detained; and for action lawfully taken to control a riot or civil disobedience.

- **Article 3: Prohibition from torture, inhumane or degrading treatment**

  This includes deliberate inhuman treatment that causes serious and cruel suffering, or treatment that causes intense physical and mental suffering, or treatment that arouses a feeling of extreme fear, anguish and inferiority capable of humiliating and debasing the victim so as to break down their moral or physical resistance.

  Where excessive force or extreme force is used or applied longer than necessary, this may amount to torture, inhumane or degrading treatment.

- **Article 8: The right to respect for private and family life**

   Article 8 states that everyone has the right to respect for their private and family life, their home and correspondence. This article has been held to include respect for an individual's physical and moral integrity. Thus, an assault may be considered a breach of article 8.

In relation to the articles above, it must be held that any use of force must be based on an honestly held belief that it is absolutely necessary and valid at the time the force is deployed.

Finally, the Code of Practice on the Police Use of Firearms and Less Lethal Weapons, which came into effect on 3 December 2003, sets out the principles in relation to the selection, testing, acquisition and use of firearms and less lethal weapons by the police. It also defines the standards for the way in which these principles should be implemented.

REFLECTIVE TASK

- *Is it necessary to have a comprehensive definition for the use of force by the police service?*

- *What are the ethical and moral challenges in having the use of force codified within legislation?*

- *Can a person who believes that it is morally and ethically wrong to use force become a police officer?*

Ethical and moral considerations in the use of force

For many people living in a democratic society, the use of force, particularly lethal force, by the police seems quite unacceptable; it goes against the notion that the police are expected to uphold the rights of all citizens and ensure that they have a right to due process. Therefore, the authorised right to employ force demands examination in relation to the necessity and legitimacy of police authority, in addition to the moral and ethical considerations in the use of force.

While several philosophical theories have been put forward in an attempt to provide justifications, the theory of *consequentialism* appears to be the theory that is most often used to justify the use of lethal force by the police (a good overview of the use of deadly force is provided in Kleinig (1996, pp108–11).

Consequentialism (a termed coined by Anscombe in 1958) refers to moral theories in that the consequences of a person's actions form the moral judgement of that conduct. Thus, if the consequences when police officers use force are considered to be good, the action is morally justified. This is often referred to as 'the ends justify the means'. This is different from both deontology and virtue ethics in that deontology assesses the right or wrong of the use of force from the character of the behaviour itself, while virtue ethics focuses on the character of the police service or police officer rather than the consequences of the use of force.

The use of force presents particular moral and ethical dilemmas, as police officers are only provided with a framework of legislation and regulation on which to base their decisions and yet their accountability in the use of force, and even more so in the use of lethal force, also rests upon their analytical, ethical and moral considerations at the time of deploying the force. Consideration of the consequences of the outcome(s) in the deployment of the use of force becomes a significant factor for officers in their accountability for their actions. Therefore, the use of force by the police is legitimised by consequentialist theory, in that the consequences of the use of force provide the greater good in terms of protecting society from harm by other individuals, thereby providing them with a safer and better quality of life. However, police officers still have to use force under the legislation and regulations that permit the use of force; it still has to be proportionate, legitimate, authorised and necessary (PLAN; see Chapter 8), as well as conform to the HRA. Therein lies the moral and ethical dilemma: police discretion may allow for one police officer to use a different level of force from another police officer, particularly in situations of crisis when decisions are made quickly to respond to changing situations. How do officers ensure that any consequences in the use of force will be for the greater good in terms of protecting society?

Since the inception of the modern police, the police themselves have been accused repeatedly of abusing their power or overstepping their authority to use force. Waddington has commented on police misuse of force, claiming that police officers operate *beyond the limits of police respectability and repeatedly at the invitational edges of corruption* (Waddington, 1999, cited in Neyroud and Beckley, 2001, p138). Neyroud and Beckley take Waddington's argument further, stating:

> *in the case of force, the problems of defining that 'edge' mean that the police are often in danger of crossing it. At one extreme this frequently exposes police officers to the accusation of assault, and at the other police officers abuse their authority and misuse force against vulnerable, powerless or minority communities.*
>
> (2001, p138)

In considering the moral and ethical dimensions of the use of force, concern about the moral implications for police officers using force must also be reflected upon. Some police officers may find the use of force abhorrent, particularly if using a higher level of force.

CASE STUDY

Andrew Kernan worked as a gardener and had suffered from schizophrenia for 15 years. On 12 July 2001, the police were called to Mr Kernan's home by his mother Marie Kernan, who had also requested a psychiatric medical team because he had become aggressive. At least four officers from Merseyside police, out of the 44 police who had arrived at the scene, entered Mrs Kernan's property but they failed to restrain Mr Kernan, who ran out into the street in his pyjamas brandishing a samurai sword.

The police negotiated with Mr Kernan for about 25 minutes and used CS gas in an attempt to control him. The police then fired two shots, the second bullet hitting Mr Kernan in the chest, and he died on the way to hospital.

Andrew Kernan had never engaged in any form of criminal behaviour and was not known to the police for being violent.

The then Home Secretary, David Blunkett, ordered a review of the incident, but over three years later on 9 December 2004, a verdict of 'lawful killing' was returned by the jury at Liverpool's District Coroner's Court and the Coroner praised the actions of the officers at the scene.

Andrew Kernan's mother has campaigned for several years about the issue of police officers being allowed to kill those who suffer from mental illness.

- *Are there special ethical and moral considerations concerning the police use of lethal force with people who are known to be suffering from mental illness?*

- *If the police use lethal force on people known to be suffering from mental illness, does this impact on the legal framework in which they have to act?*

- *How would you assess the 'severity of harm' that Andrew Kernan may have posed to the community in this situation?*

Types of legitimate force used by the police

The police are empowered with a range of coercive resources when considering deploying force. These resources represent the continuum of force that the police can legitimately use, from gentle coercion to lethal force. Such resources include physical force, batons, handcuffs, incapacitant spray, taser guns, dogs and firearms (McKenzie, 2000). There are three key issues in considering whether deployment of force by police officers is reasonable and justified: whether the force was used to maintain order and prevent harm and was not used maliciously; whether the force used was excessive or unreasonable in the given situation; and whether the force was applied for the right reasons and not influenced by discriminatory bias, self-serving interests or other factors.

Kleinig has identified five factors that are relevant to the ethical assessment of the use of force.

Five factors for the ethical assessment of the use of force

1. Intention

The intention to use force must be to achieve a specific outcome, normally to maintain order or prevent harm. The measure of the force must be properly applied in order to secure the desired outcome and no more. Therefore, there should be no intent to apply any additional force for malicious purposes, such as self-serving interests or 'teaching them a lesson'.

2. Seemliness

The use of force must also be seen as seemly and in keeping with accepted standards appropriate to the circumstances. The receiver at the end of the use of force must not be treated inhumanely or callously; they must be treated with what is decently acceptable.

3. Proportionality

The amount of force used must be proportionate to the serious of the incident or offence being committed.

4. Minimisation

The least amount of force must be used in order to achieve the desired outcome. The police have a range of resources available and need to use the one that is least harmful, least intrusive, least invasive and least disturbing to the receiver of the force.

5. Practicability

The force used must be capable of being deployed successfully in order to achieve the desired outcome. Force is required in many cases to protect the public or to apprehend a dangerous criminal; however, when force is applied in situations that do not require force but a different policing approach, it does not merit justification. The policing of protests is an example where practicability may be tested and challenged. On the one hand, community policing encourages a soft approach of engaging with the public and yet, on the other, the policing of public peace often requires a paramilitary approach that is viewed as a hard style of policing that often appears to be forceful and more adversarial.

(Adapted from Kleinig, 1996, pp99–102)

If Kleinig's five factors provide an ethical appraisal for the use of acceptable force, Neyroud and Beckley (2001) contend that this is just part of the justification for the use of force and they identify a further three issues:

- the methods of force deployed;
- the competence of the officer;
- the strategic, legal and societal framework (this has been discussed throughout the chapter).

Methods of force

Neyroud and Beckley (2001) argue that there is a range of coercive resources that represent a continuum of force from communication to lethal options. While the five factors of Kleinig's ethical assessment must be applied in each case to ensure that the force is justified, Neyroud and Beckley state that, in incidents where use of force is deployed, these incidents often escalate through that continuum. Therefore, an incident may commence with communication between a police officer and suspect, and escalate to use of physical force and a taser gun being deployed. The decision at which level the force is deployed is dependent on the behaviour of the suspect, the situational context, the information known about the suspect, the suspect's response to initial police contact and the coercive resources available to the police officers. But the level of force must be absolutely necessary and proportionate to the situation.

The competence of the officer

It has been argued that emphasis on the skills required for officers using force is not necessarily one of being highly skilled in the specific deployment of a particular type of force, but rather one of competence in being able to analyse and appraise the situation, being able to communicate well and being able to assess the minimal force required to bring about the desired outcome. The measure of success in an incident involving the use of force is not how well or skilfully the force has been deployed, but if that force has been reasonable in the context of the situation. Neyroud and Beckley (2001) refer to this as the 'conflict resolution' model, and suggest that this model requires a shift in the *traditional method of control systems towards a more professional model, encouraging high skills through accreditation, mentoring, peer coaching and supervisor monitoring* (2001, p141). The importance of developing more competent officers whose skills allow them to consider the situation in relation to the suspect and the context, and whether a different approach may be required to achieve the desired outcome, rather than officers whose skills are merely to be able to deploy force tactics skilfully and expertly without any real understanding of the context of the incident, may refocus the traditional disciplinary approach for police officers who are accused of using 'excessive force' towards a more compliant, professional standards model.

However, the deployment of reasonable force is primarily linked to assessing and ensuring the safety of the police officer, his or her colleagues and the public in the particular situation being policed. To an extent, an officer's own safety training will inform his or her reaction to assessing the situation. If the officer does not feel competent in deploying the minimum use of force, such as communication, handcuffs and incapacitant spray, he or she will defer to the highest level of force that the officer feels competent to use in order to control the situation. Therefore, officer training safety skills must be appropriate, proper and up to date.

The strategic, legal and societal framework

Neyroud and Beckley (2001) state that the police service needs to provide a clear framework in relation to policy and standards in the use of force that considers the minimum deployment of force, officer safety, and effective monitoring and review processes. In addition, an efficient consultation and complaints system is required together with a clear legal framework (Neyroud and Beckley, 2001). These issues have been discussed throughout the chapter.

REFLECTIVE TASK

HMIC produced a review of officer safety training in April 2007 called Safety Matters. *This report can be located on the HMIC website: www.hmic.gov.uk/sitecollectiondocuments/thematics/thm_20070331.pdf*

Access the report and consider the following issues.

- *Do police officers receive appropriate and sufficient officer safety training?*

- *What are the moral obligations of the police service in ensuring that police officers provide sufficient training to allow officers to develop effective skills and knowledge in deploying force?*

- *What are the ethical implications for both police officers and the police service from the findings of this report?*

In adhering to and maintaining the legal requirements for applying force and upholding the social contract mandate that authorises the police to legitimately use force on behalf of society, the police have developed a range of tools to allow different levels in the use of force to achieve the desired outcomes. However, the ultimate deployment of force by the police is that of lethal force.

Lethal force

Kleinig (1996) has argued that the use of lethal force is problematic in that it is final and a tragic invasion of an individual's most basic rights and interests. In deploying lethal force, the police have failed not only in allowing the deceased the right to a fair trial, which is arguably one of their key roles within the criminal justice system, but also in not achieving the desired outcome by any other means. Whether excessive use of force, or use of excessive force, has been used is always a matter for debate following the use of lethal force by the police. This debate is significant as it challenges whether the use of force deployed was either illegal or unnecessary. Illegal use of force is where officers use lethal force that exceeds the threshold of their office. Unnecessary force is the use of force, either intentionally or unintentionally, that proves incapable of dealing with the incident and, therefore, the use of force without necessarily having to in order to control the situation (Fyfe, 1986).

The police, however, are not necessarily protected from disapprobation for the use of fatal force; their immunity is subject to the circumstances of the particular incident.

Police use of firearms

The ultimate use of force by police officers in England and Wales is the deployment of firearms. The police strategy in England and Wales is policing by consent and it has been held that the police should not be routinely armed to maintain the character of policing by consent. If the police were to be routinely armed, not only would it legitimise the weapon as a symbol of force by the state, but it would undermine the principle of community policing.

The latest figures for firearm incidents and firearm discharges from 1 April 2008 to 31 March 2009 are shown in Table 6.2.

Although there were almost 20,000 police operations in which firearms were authorised, there were only four incidents where the police discharged a firearm. Thus, the number of incidents in which firearms are used remains extremely small in England and Wales. The use of firearms as the ultimate in lethal force remains the last resort and is only considered when there is a serious risk to the public or the police.

Table 6.2 Firearm incidents and discharges, 2008–09

Number of police officers who are trained and authorised to use firearms	6,868
Number of police operations in which firearms were authorised	19,951
Number of operations involving armed response vehicles	16,564
Incidents where police discharged a conventional firearm	4

Source: Home Office (2010, p1).

CASE STUDY

Henry (Harry) Stanley was a 46-year-old Scottish painter and decorator who lived in Hackney, East London. On 22 September 1999, he had gone to his brother's to help him repair a broken table leg. He had taken the table leg home with him wrapped in a black plastic bag. On his way home he stopped at a pub and, by the time he left, someone had called the police to say that an Irishman was in the pub with a gun wrapped in a bag.

CASE STUDY continued

Mr Stanley was shot just yards away from his home by two police officers who claimed that he turned around to face them and assumed a classic firing position. Fearing they would be shot, the police officers opened fire at Mr Stanley, killing him. Mr Stanley had only come out of hospital a week earlier after having had a cancerous tumour removed from his bowel and therefore would be walking quite slowly.

The first inquest returned an open verdict, but the Coroner had instructed the jury that they could only return a verdict of unlawful killing or open verdict. Mr Stanley's widow petitioned the High Court and obtained a judicial review of the first inquest. At the judicial review, ballistics experts challenged the initial police officers' statement that Mr Stanley had turned around to face them, by presenting evidence that showed the fatal bullet had entered the back of his head and not the front, thus he was facing away from the police officers when they shot him.

In November 2004, a new jury returned the verdict of unlawful killing and the two officers were suspended from police duties. In protest at their suspension, over 100 police officers returned their weapons to the police stores. The suspension was lifted shortly afterwards.

In May 2005, the High Court overturned the verdict of unlawful killing, citing insufficient evidence, and returned the original open verdict. The judge also concluded that no further inquest should be held but did support reform of the inquest system.

However, in June 2005, the two officers involved in the shooting were arrested and interviewed following an independent investigation by Surrey Police, which disclosed new evidence, but in October 2005 the Crown Prosecution Service did not press charges as it felt that the evidence was insufficient to invalidate the officers' defence of acting in self-defence.

REFLECTIVE TASK

- *Did the use of force in the above case study comply and conform to PLAN – was it proportionate, legitimate, authorised and necessary?*

- *Was the use and level of force acceptable in this case?*

- *How would article 2 of the HRA support or refute that the use of force was lawful in this case?*

- *How would Neyroud and Beckley's (2001) consideration of the 'competence of the officer' be applied to the officers involved in the shooting?*

Excessive use of force

Kleinig (1996) succinctly observes that, while the police are authorised to use force, there is little consideration by the police themselves as to what level and type of force is necessary or justified; it is left to others to demonstrate that a particular use of force was excessive or unjustified. Therefore, there is an element of subjectivity when considering excessive use of force.

The argument is not that force should not be used in policing; rather, there are times when it is necessary for police to deploy force, sometimes to the extent that the police may have to consider deploying lethal force to protect others. There is the expectation that, if the police have been authorised to use force on behalf of the state, this needs to be carefully regulated and monitored. The term 'excessive' in its application in the use of force is in itself problematic. As Belur (2010) maintains, consideration of the term 'excessive' involves value judgements and various criteria will apply in determining whether use of force was excessive depending on who is making the judgement. She states that judges will apply the legal understanding of the term 'excessive', whereas police managers will apply professional standards criteria and human rights activists will apply ethical standards (Belur, 2010).

It is also argued that there is a distinction between the terms 'excessive use of force' and 'the use of excessive force'. The first implies that force was used in too many incidents, while the second is that more force than needed was used to gain compliance in any given incident (Adams, 1995, quoted in Terrill, 2001, p22).

Klockers (1996) adds to the debate by proposing that there should be one definition to judge the extent of the force used and whether it was excessive. This would provide a standard by which to measure the concept of 'excessive'. He states that *excessive force should be defined as the use of more force than a highly skilled police officer would find necessary to use in that particular situation* (1996, p8).

REFLECTIVE TASK

The shooting of Jean Charles de Menezes in July 2007 has been one of the most controversial lethal uses of force by the police to date. The IPCC launched two investigations referred to as Stockwell 1 and Stockwell 2.

Access these reports from the IPCC website:

- *www.ipcc.gov.uk/Documents/stockwell_one.pdf www.ipcc.gov.uk/Documents/ipcc_ stockwell_2.pdf*

Discuss the findings and recommendations from these reports in relation to the ethical use of lethal force.

C H A P T E R   S U M M A R Y

This chapter has considered how ethics are applied and understood in the use of force by police officers. It examined how force is considered as a core function of policing and how the police are authorised to use force in carrying out their role by the state. Although the police are authorised to use force, there is legislation to ensure that such force is deployed reasonably, proportionately, legitimately and only when necessary. In addition, use of force has to be compliant with the HRA to ensure its lawfulness. The chapter explored some ethical assessment tools when using force and how these tools provide justification when force has been deployed. The use of lethal force was discussed in relation to police firearms and used a range of case studies and tasks to underline the ethical and moral implications.

REFERENCES

Anscombe, G (1958) Modern Moral Philosophy. *Philosophy*, 33(124).

Belur, J (2010) *Permission to Shoot: Police use of deadly force in democracies*. New York: Springer.

Bittner, E (1991) The Functions of Police in Modern Society, in Klockers, C and Mastrofski, S (eds) *Thinking about Police*. New York: McGraw-Hill.

Explained.At (2011) Metropolitan Police Service Explained. Online at http://everything.explained.at/ Metropolitan_Police_Service (accessed 22 November 2011).

Fyfe, J (1986) The 'Split-second Syndrome' and Other Determinants of Police Violence, in Campbell, AT and Gibbs, J (eds) *Violent Transactions*. New York: Basil Blackwell.

Home Office (2010) *Statistics on Police Use of Firearms 2008–09*. London: Home Office. Online at http://tna.europarchive.org/20100419081706/http://wwwpolice.homeoffice.gov.uk.documents/ Police-firearms-2008–09.html (accessed 22 November 2011).

IACP (International Association of Chiefs of Police) (2001) *Police Use of Force in America 2001*. Alexandria, VA: IAPC.

Kleinig, J (1996) *The Ethics of Policing*, Cambridge: Cambridge University Press.

Klockers, CB (1996) A Theory of Excess Force and its Control, in Geller, W and Toch, H (eds) *Policy Violence: Understanding and controlling police use of force*. New Haven, CT, and London: Yale University Press.

Manning, PK (1977) *Police Work: The social organisation of policing*. Cambridge, MA: MIT Press.

McKenzie, I (2000) Policing Force: Rules, hierarchies and consequences, in Leishman, B, Loveday, B and Savage, S (eds) *Core Issues in Policing*, 2nd edition. Harlow: Longman.

McLaughlin, V (1992) *Police and the Use of Force: The Savannah Study*. Westport, CT: Praeger.

Neyroud, P and Beckley, A (2001) *Policing, Ethics and Human Rights*. Cullompton: Willan.

Sherman, L (1982) *Ethics in Criminal Justice Education*. New York: Hastings Center.

Skolnick, J and Fyfe, J (1993) *Above the Law: Police and excessive use of force*. New York: Free Press.

Terrill, W (2001) *Police Coercion: Application of the force continuum*. New York: LFB.

Waddington, PAJ (1999) *Policing Citizens: Authority and rights.* London: UCL Press.

www.hmic.gov.uk – Her Majesty's Inspectorate of Constabulary

www.ipcc.gov.uk – Independent Police Complaints Commission

www.legislation.gov.uk – most types of legislation, including the Human Rights Act 1998

7 An ethical approach to policing public disorder

CHAPTER OBJECTIVES

By the end of this chapter you should be able to:

- recognise how ethics and morals are considered in policing disorders;
- understand how legislation relating to the use of public order provides ethical guidelines;
- identify the ethical theories and models that can be applied to policing public order;
- appreciate the changing contexts of public disorder and, in particular, the political dimension of such disorder and the challenges for maintaining ethical practice.

LINKS TO STANDARDS

This chapter provides opportunities for links with the following Skills for Justice, National Occupational Standards (NOS) for Policing and Law Enforcement 2008.

AE1.1	Maintain and develop your own knowledge, skills and competence.
CA1	Use law enforcement actions in a fair and justified way.
CC201	Formulate, monitor and review tactical plans to achieve strategic objectives for public order operations.
CC7	Prepare for, monitor and maintain law enforcement operations.
GC10	Manage conflict.
HA1	Manage your own resources.
HA2	Manage your own resources and professional development.
POL1A1	Use police action in a fair and justified way.
POL2C2	Prepare for, and participate in, planned policing operations
POL2C4	Minimise and deal with aggressive and abusive behaviour.

With the introduction of the Qualification and Credit Framework (QCF), it is likely that the term 'National Occupational Standards' will change. At the time of writing it is not clear what the new title will be, although it is known that some organisations will use the term 'QCF assessment units'.

Links to current NOS are provided at the start of each chapter; however, it should be noted that these are currently subject to review and it is recommended that you visit the Skills for Justice website to check the currency of all the NOS provided: www.skillsforjustice-nosfinder.com.

Introduction

One of the principles of the modern police service, as attributed to Sir Robert Peel, states that the basic mission for which the police exist is to prevent crime and *disorder*. A further four out of the nine principles credited to Peel can be specifically related to the policing of disorder, namely that the ability of the police in performing their duties is dependent upon public approval of police actions; that the extent of physical force used must be only that necessary to secure or restore order when other non-physical attempts have failed; that public cooperation diminishes in proportion to the necessity of the use of physical force; and the test of police efficiency is the *absence of crime and disorder and not the visible evidence of police action dealing with it* (Grieve et al., 2007, p37).

Public order policing is often characterised by visible, large-scale deployment of officers, frequently managed through a military-style, command-and-control format. These officers can be accompanied by a range of tools such as shields, truncheons, horses and dogs, with an emphasis on maintaining control as much as enforcing the law (Waddington, 2007). However, despite the media portrayal of public order policing as being confrontational and forceful, events that include violence and disorder leading to confrontation between the police and protestors that result in arrests are infrequent.

Yet, despite the fact that few events lead to confrontation between police and protest groups, modern policing has, to a considerable extent, been defined by the policing of public disorder. From policing the Cold Bath Fields in 1833 to the G-20 Summit in London in 2009, when an innocent member of the public died apparently as a result of police action, the topic of ethical and value-based policing of public disorder has been long debated (HMIC, 2009a, 2009b, 2011).

The historical context of ethical public order policing

The newly formed Metropolitan Police Force was involved in policing riots and crowd control from its inception in 1829. Indeed, Reiner (1985) postulates that the police service was created in response to concerns relating to public order and unrest. Although initially experimenting with passive control methods, the Metropolitan Police rapidly employed more physical force and baton charges were used in 1830 in the Swing Riots. However, the early development of crowd control tactics can be traced to the Cold Bath Fields incident in 1833. This incident started with what was meant to be a political meeting and ended up as a disastrous riot in which three police officers were stabbed, one of whom, PC Robert Culley, was fatally wounded. Three thousand police officers, batons drawn, descended upon the thousand attendees at the meeting in a confrontation that resulted in several injuries to both police and protestors.

The inquest into the death of PC Culley, who was stabbed through the heart, returned a verdict of 'justifiable homicide' and the jurors were treated as heroes as the result of their decision. The jury was able to justify its decision on the fact that the crowd had not been ordered to disperse under the Riot Act 1714 and, in particular, that the 'conduct of the police was ferocious, brutal, and unprovoked by the people'. Notably, the jury foreman and his fellow jurymen received medallions sent by an anonymous donor; one side contained all the names of the jurors and the message 'We shall be recompensed, the resurrection of the just' and the other side was engraved with 'In honour of the men who notably withstood the dictation of the coroner; independent, and conscientious, discharge of their duty; promoted a continued reliance upon the laws under the protection of a British jury'. The verdict was overturned by the High Court and public opinion started to turn when newspapers publicised the plight of PC Culley's widow (Open University, 2009).

Nonetheless, the early experience of managing public disorder was to set the way the police were to respond and deal with public disorder events for the following 180 years. Despite the number of violent disorders since 1829, only two police officers have been killed in England and Wales as a result of riots: PC Culley at the Cold Bath Fields riots in 1833 and PC Keith Blakelock, who was killed at Broadwater Farm in 1985. However, there have been several protestors whose deaths have been attributed to police action during public disorder events: David Moore, a disabled 23-year-old, was knocked down and killed by a police landrover while police were dispersing rioters in Toxteth in July 1981; Blair Peach died from head injuries in a demonstration in Southall in April 1979; and Ian Tomlinson was pushed and struck by a baton as he walked past police officers on his way home during the G20 Summit protests in April 2009.

REFLECTIVE TASK

The HMIC report, Adapting to Protest *(2009a), states:*

> Presently, public order training focuses largely on dealing with disorder and unrest, with officers in NATO helmets, wearing protective equipment and carrying shields. In relatively few instances are police deployed in this manner and, where they are, this is towards the limits of the spectrum of crowd management. Additionally, officers bring to public order training their individual officer safety skills, developed for everyday policing. Bringing the two skill sets together has highlighted contrasting approaches to a graduated response to the use of force and associated human rights considerations, which are well evidenced and documented in officer safety training but markedly less well integrated into public order training.
>
> Overall, this current position raises questions about the preparedness of officers to display a graduation and range of policing styles and tactics, all of which, at different times, may be appropriate for policing protest.
>
> *(HMIC, 2009, p9)*

- *Discuss the above statement in relation to public order training and the different policing skills that are required for such training.*

- *Consider what ethical issues could be taken into account and included in the training for public order.*

Policing public disorder is very different from other policing tasks. Waddington (2007) articulates that day-to-day policing tends to be a solitary and even invisible endeavour where officers engage with the public as individuals. In contrast, policing public order requires officers to act as a group, usually adopting specific tactics in crowd control (Waddington, 2007). The media image of policing large gatherings often portrays *angry confrontations, baton-wielding police, tear gas, 'messy' arrests and bloodied combatants* (2007, p375). This image of riot gear-clad officers engaged in forceful confrontation assisted by an array of tools such as dogs, horses, truncheons and shields, while powerful, does not represent reality.

Waddington (2007) argues that this image is misleading at many levels. Most demonstrations and protests are policed by officers in regular uniform and there are only a few arrests and rarely violence. Indeed, the Metropolitan Police Service recorded over 5,324 protests in London during 2008 alone, the majority of which were peaceful (HMIC, 2009a). These protests were mainly processions, which are notifiable under the Public Order Act 1986, although there are significantly more static assemblies that are not notified even if police officers are in attendance. If violence does erupt that requires suppression, it occurs in a range of contexts including football hooliganism, street carnivals and events associated with youth culture (Waddington, 2007).

Furthermore, Waddington (2007) asserts that there is a difference between policing public order and policing public disorder. He argues that most commentators adopt an orthodox view when commenting on policing crowds and that they focus merely on the policing of disorder. What Waddington claims is that the police engage in 'public order policing', in which the police endeavour to avoid confrontation and disorder with protestors. In maintaining a 'policing by consent' approach, the police seek to avoid using powers under the Public Order Act 1986 and prefer to negotiate with protestors rather than arrest them, often preventing potential confrontation that creates disorder:

> *There is often ample legal justification for arresting protestors, but senior commanders actively restrain their subordinates from taking such a course of action for fear of wider consequences.*
>
> (Waddington, 1998)

It is only when the policing public order strategy fails and disorder occurs that policing tactics change to one of policing disorder. This can involve a more paramilitary style of policing – one that is characterised by police wearing riot gear, often accompanied by horses and dogs, and using specific tactics that have been developed to control and manage disorder – suppressing protestors by force rather than persuasion.

Legislation pertaining to public order

There are a number of laws that govern how the police control and manage public order and these are detailed below.

Breach of the peace

In England, Wales and Northern Ireland, breach of the peace is descended from the 1361 Justices of the Peace Act. A breach of the peace is not an offence in that it is not punishable by either a fine or imprisonment within statute law. Police officers are permitted to arrest a citizen if they believe that a breach of the peace has occurred or is about to occur. The Act originally referred to riotous behaviour that may have disturbed the peace of the King; its modern interpretation defines it as when harm is done, or likely to be done, to a person or property, or a person is fearful of being harmed through an assault or riot or lawful assembly or some other form of disturbance. It is also used when a police officer also believes that someone is likely to be the victim of a breach of the peace or an act of violence. The only sanction that can be imposed by a court is to bind over the offender to keep the peace and, should the offender refuse such binding, they may be committed to custody under the Magistrates Court Act 1980 (Jerrard, 2003).

The Riot Act 1714

The Riot Act of 1714 authorised local authorities to declare a group of 12 or more people to be unlawfully assembled and gave them the power to disperse them or issue further punitive sanctions. The last record of the Riot Act being enacted in the UK was at a bonfire festival in 1929, although it was read out in 1919 during the two police strikes of 1918 and 1919. Over one thousand police officers from Birkenhead, Liverpool and Bootle joined the strike. Concerned that public civil unrest would occur, the army was mobilised to police the area. Indeed, rioting and looting were rife and, as the Riot Act was read out, 700 soldiers were drafted in to support the remaining police who were not on strike to maintain order. This Act remained as a statute until it was repealed by section 10 of the Criminal Law Act 1967, as it fell into disuse (History House, 2011). However, the Riot Act is still used in India, where the Collector/Magistrate can still give authority to clear the streets.

Public Order Act 1936

The Public Order Act 1936 was passed as an attempt to control extremist political movements that began to emerge in the 1930s, such as the British Union of Fascists. The Act banned the wearing of any political uniforms in a public place or at a public meeting and required the permission of the police for political marches to take place.

The Act was used extensively against the Irish Republican Army (IRA) and Sinn Fein demonstrations of the 1970s, although in law the Act did not apply to Northern Ireland as the latter was subject to the Northern Ireland Emergency Powers legislation. For example, in 1974, 12 people were fined £50 each for wearing the black berets of the Sinn Fein uniform at Speakers Corners during a Sinn Fein rally. However, the Public Order Act 1936 was considered ineffective at dealing with public disorder and violence and was super-seded by the Public Order Act 1986 (Townshend, 1993).

Public Order Act 1986

The Public Order Act 1986 introduced greater measures to control disorder from demonstrations and protests. The Act has attracted criticism for failing to balance the rights of individuals in relation to freedom of assembly and freedom of expression. The Act requires protest groups intending to march or protest to give notification to the police at least six days in advance of the event taking place, allowing the police to prohibit or place conditions on the event if they believe serious public disorder, serious criminal damage or serious disruption to the life of the community are likely to occur. However, any conditions imposed by the police are limited to specifying the number of people who may take part, the location and how long the event is to take place. It is only with the authority of the Secretary of State that the police can prohibit a march.

In addition, the Act creates new offences under sections 4 and 5 for behaviour or actions with intent to cause harassment, alarm or distress, including actions that incite racial hatred (Sanders and Young, 2003; Townshend, 1993).

Criminal Justice and Public Order Act 1994

This Act increased further sanctions against disruptive trespass, squatters and unauthorised campers, criminalising previously what were civil offences. This was designed to deal with mass trespass by those planning to hold music festivals, as well as mass trespass on to construction sites or other places of protest. It has had a significant effect on many forms of protest, including environmental protest and anti-hunt demonstrations.

Section 60 of this Act also gives police the right to search people in a defined area at a specific time when they have good reason to believe that there is the possibility of serious violence, or that a serious incident involving violence has taken place and that the person is carrying a dangerous object or offensive weapon to commit crime, or has committed that crime.

Public Order Acts and competing rights

Policing public order requires a fine balance between the competing rights of the protestors and the rights of those who have opposing views and the rights of those members of the community who reside in the area of protest:

> *public order law and the policing of it involves balancing the rights of individuals with one another against wider entitlements and requirements of society – a task that, in practical terms, can seem like trying to satisfy the insatiable.*
>
> (Hutton and McKinnon, 2008, p138)

Commentators, including non-governmental organisations (NGOs) such as Liberty, have been particularly critical of the way some public order events have been policed, stating that certain sections of Public Order Acts are used to stifle protest or free speech.

Section 5 of the Public Order Act 1986 criminalises 'threatening, abusive or insulting words' or behaviour in certain circumstances.

Case study 1
A young man was protesting outside the Church of Scientology in London and the police issued him with a summons for refusing to take down his banner, which stated that 'Scientology is not a religion, it is a dangerous cult.' The police claimed that the use of the word 'cult' violated section 5 of the Public Disorder Act.

Case study 2
The police arrested a protestor at a rally for wearing a picture of a cartoon depicting the prophet Mohammed. The police explained that the arrest was made during a very tense period and a person came forward to complain about the cartoon, stating that they felt it would cause a breach of the peace and that they were personally offended by it. It was at that point that the police arrested the protestor.

REFLECTIVE TASK

Using the case studies above, consider the following.

- *Are police powers under section 5 of the Public Order Act ill-defined?*
- *Does the definition of section 5 take into account the competing rights of the differing and opposing views held within society?*
- *Could the police inappropriately use the Act in order to facilitate greater control of protest groups at the expense of infringing their human rights?*

There is an inextricable and deep relationship between the right to protest and the right to free speech. Some protests will inevitably cause offence to others. These create unique challenges for the police and how they ethically approach and manage public order events.

The ethical challenges of policing public order

The 1960s saw a change in society's attitudes towards the police. The legitimate authority of the police was increasingly questioned and challenged, particularly in protests and demonstrations. The 1970s and 1980s witnessed a period of social uprising, starting with the miners' strike and leading to the 'winter of discontent'. High unemployment, economic stagnation and rising inflation were followed by a period of riots and disturbance. This redefined the relationship between the police and the public.

Sir Robert Mark, the Commissioner of the Metropolitan Police Service from 1972 until 1977, argued at that time that the police must be 'seen to lose' in order to maintain public legitimacy. Police leaders were supported by the then Prime Minister, Margaret Thatcher, in adopting this approach. Part of this arose because of the high cost of injuries to police officers in the Brixton Riots and the need to protect them, and part from a deliberate re-examination of police tactics, which resulted in the reintroduction to mainland UK of the tactics that were only used in Northern Ireland or in the Commonwealth (for example, Hong Kong). There was a conscious reinvention of police tactics and a refocus on police controlling crowds. This change was also encouraged by the challenge of dealing with football violence, which was endemic at the time. The high-water mark of this approach was the miners' strike:

> *Instead of police officers being distributed randomly along the picket line as was seen in the 1960s, the police were now fully equipped, wearing riot helmets, shields and operating in squads. This clearly demonstrates a move away from low profile tactics to ruling with an iron fist. Further tactics have been developed which mean the police using incapacitating spray, shields, 'kettling', bean bags and tear gas.*
>
> (Rogers et al., 2011, p307)

This model of policing, which Jefferson (1990) described as 'paramilitary', was symbolised in the Metropolitan Police Special Patrol Group (SPG), which was created in 1965 to provide a mobile response squad to combat public disorder in London. It was only in 1973 that the public became aware of the SPG, when it responded to an incident at India House in which two young Pakistani men were shot dead for holding a number of people hostage with guns that looked sufficiently real to intimidate the hostages. However, concerns about the SPG increased steadily throughout the 1970s, but most complaints were voiced by the Black community about local raids and stop and search. In 1975, the SPG stopped over 65,000 people but only arrested 4,125. However, in the mid-1970s the nature of demonstrations changed as anti-fascists and anti-racist groups engaged in more violent protests, with the police being seen as legitimate targets for violence by the protestors. This was the case in the Red Lion Square disorders in 1974, in which a group of liberal political parties protested against the National Front holding a meeting in London. An international Marxist group broke away from the protest group and endeavoured to confront the National Front. During the protest a student and member of this Marxist group, Kevin Gately, died, allegedly as the result of injuries he received. Lord Scarman said in his report that this could be a possibility, but that it was impossible to definitively attribute the death to a blow to the head from a police truncheon. Gately was the first person to be killed at a public political demonstration in the UK for 55 years. It was during this and the policing of a mass mobilisation against the fascists in Lewisham in 1977, that the tactics of the SPG became exposed.

The death of Blair Peach

The background of the demonstration that culminated in a riot was the decision by members of the National Front to hold an election meeting in Southall, London, in 1979. This area was predominantly inhabited by members of the Asian community, but the National Front deliberately chose this area in an attempt to gain publicity and cause disruption to the local community. Throughout the day, which was wet and cold, there were many incidents including scuffles and throwing of objects, mainly at police officers, as they were accused by the Asian community of protecting the National Front. The police were duty bound to do so under the Representation of the People Act, since it was an 'election meeting'.

As the tension mounted, crowds of young Asians and white people turned their anger towards the police. Comments of 'get the pigs' and 'the police are the National Front in uniform' were heard coming from the protestors. Flares were also fired from the upstairs windows of a nearby house. Almost 2,800 officers were on duty, notably almost one for each demonstrator, and their role was to keep the two sets of protestors apart. During the ensuing riots, about 120 police officers were injured, along with almost 100 protestors and members of the community. During the day, Blair Peach, a New Zealand-born teacher, was struck on the head and later died in hospital.

In June 2000, the Metropolitan Police Service conducted an inquiry into the death of Blair Peach and, as part of that inquiry, found that a search of the SPG officers who were known to be in the area where Peach was struck had been conducted. This search had revealed an arsenal of non-police-issued weapons, such as a leather-cased metal truncheon with a knotted thong, a metal truncheon with lead weighting, a knife, crowbars and sledgehammer handles. One locker contained material that indicated the police officer was a Nazi supporter. The inquiry ensured that recruitment to the SPG was suspended while a review of the group was undertaken. This review disbanded the SPG and replaced it with District Support Units, which had a greater decentralised command structure. The review limited the time that officers could serve on these units; however, their accountability still remained obscure.

After reading the above case study, consider the following.

- *What are the ethical challenges of having specific police units for dealing with public order?*

- *Would placing limitations on the length of time that a police officer can serve on a specialised public order unit influence the ethical behaviour of police officers?*

- *Would greater accountability help promote fair and principled behaviour in policing public order?*

- *What are the considerations for the police in balancing the rights of competing protest groups against the rights of the community in which the protest is to take place, while maintaining liberty and security for each group?*

Waddington (2003) has argued that the greatest challenge to public order during the twentieth century came from the extremes of the political spectrum: the labour movement and the fascist movement. In particular, the miners' strike in 1984 epitomised the discord between the militant trade unions and the ideology of the Thatcher government at the time. As the traditional industries, such as mining, the steelworks and printing, started to decline, the government was embracing a free and competitive market. The miners' strike of 1984–85 came to represent the symbolic struggle of that time, ending in the defeat of the miners and a breaking of trade union power, enabling the conservative free state market to advance.

Thousands of officers were drafted in to police the strike, and for the first time in policing industrial disputes, they were equipped with riot gear and used aggressive tactics (Waddington, 2003). The defeat of the miners' strike broke the hold that the trade unions had and there were few further political industrial disputes that required the same level of policing. The policing of the miners' strike was characterised by the mobilisation of mutual aid, where police officers from many forces came to support and help their colleagues in the force area where the strike occurred. In addition, the policing tactics became aggressive with more forceful tactics.

The ethical challenges of policing public order in the twenty-first century

Policing public order in the twenty-first century has thus far been characterised by a series of key reports from HMIC: *Adapting to Protest* (2009a), *Adapting to Protest: Nurturing the British model* (2009b) and *Policing Public Order* (2011).

Adapting to Protest (2009a) was commissioned as a result of the G20 protests in late March and April 2009, which were held by a number of groups protesting over major global political issues. Although the majority of protests were peaceful, there were a number of violent and criminal incidents. The police were heavily criticised for 'kettling' protestors (a public order tactic that involves the containment of protestors for a period of time). There were also a number of serious allegations of police misconduct, some of which were recorded by either the media or protestors on mobile telephones. An innocent bystander, Ian Tomlinson, died shortly after being hit and pushed to the ground by a police officer and the subsequent inquest found that he had been unlawfully killed (Inquest, 2011).

The report (2009a) concluded that there was a lack of clarity around the use of force in public order policing, and it recommended that the relevant human rights principles be incorporated into police training for public order, and in particular the use of force in such situations. *Adapting to Protest: Nurturing the British Model* (2009b) further highlighted that there was little guidance or discussion around either the legislation or the legal implications of public order techniques. It also drew attention to the police manual, *The Public Order Standards, Tactics and Training Manual*, designed to provide practical guidance on public order techniques, which lacked effective guidance on levels of force or threshold tests that should be met before force is used.

The HMIC report, *Policing Public Order* (2011), identified that the patterns and nature of protests had evolved since the 1980s in terms of greater frequency, the number of protestors at any one event and the spread of disruption, which all have the propensity to cause even greater disruption, including violence. The report called for the police to be more 'agile' in their response as modern protests become more 'inherently messy':

> Police tactics must be as adaptable as possible to the circumstances and the challenge of striking the right balance between competing rights is a difficult judgement call.
>
> (HMIC, 2011, p3)

While the report acknowledges the challenges of policing protests, it also stated that the police must actively work to ensure that people were able to protest.

The use of social media and mobile telephone communication enables protests to be organised in a matter of hours, and protestors can occupy places and spaces within a matter of minutes. The focus for the protest can also change rapidly, with incitement of violence, looting and other forms of criminality (HMIC, 2011). The report further reinforced the fact that protest groups can still comprise several sub-groups, which include genuine protestors intent on peaceful protest and also those intent on criminality. This creates specific challenges for the police and requires a high degree of adaptability, but an adaptability that is underpinned by ethics, integrity and public consent while maintaining the liberties of protestors alongside the need to maintain order.

Collectively, these reports called for a much more considered response to the policing of public order, with emphasis on training about human rights within public order situations, more communication with protestors, understanding proportionality of force and accountability of action. The greater use of social networking and mobile telephones means that police actions are being recorded in 'real time' by protestors and bystanders, which could be used as evidence of police behaviour.

CASE STUDY

The England Riots, August 2011

Following a peaceful protest on 6 August 2011 in response to the shooting of Mark Duggan by the Metropolitan Police Service two days earlier, a series of riots occurred. As a result of these riots, between 6 and 10 August 2011, over 20 districts in London and several other cities and towns in England suffered widespread disorder.

These riots were characterised by violence, looting and arson attacks of unprecedented levels. As a result, the Home Secretary ordered that all police leave should be cancelled and Parliament was recalled from its summer recess for a day on 11 August to debate the situation.

Five people died and at least 16 others were injured as a direct result of related violent acts; 186 police officers were injured. Police action has been blamed for the initial riot, and the subsequent police reaction was criticised as being neither appropriate nor sufficiently effective.

As of 12 September 2011, 1,715 people had appeared before the courts with almost two-thirds being remanded in custody (Ministry of Justice, 2011).

REFLECTIVE TASK

Finding appropriate resources from the internet, reports and books, consider the following.

- *There were numerous calls from the public, politicians and media for the police to deploy water cannons, plastic bullets and baton rounds. Senior police leaders rejected these calls, saying that deploying such tactics for public disorder would undermine the ethos of British policing: that of policing by consent. Explain if, and how, more forceful tactics may be ethically deployed by the police.*

- *The police are expected to uphold the law and yet, in some cases of public order, the protestors commit crimes against the police, including violence, spitting at officers and making discriminatory and racist remarks and chants. What strategies might be useful in these situations to ensure police officers maintain their integrity and respond proportionately and fairly?*

- *In the G20 protests the police were accused of applying too much force and being too aggressive in some circumstances; however, the police were also blamed for not intervening forcefully in the situation and therefore being ineffective. In the ethical strategies you have identified above, how could you demonstrate whether police tactics are appropriate for a particular situation? What would be the indicators that a strategy was effective or not? If you had to consider revising a strategy to adjust to the changing nature of a particular protest, how could you ensure that integrity was maintained during the change of tactics/strategy for controlling and managing a protest? Could an ethical decision-making model such as the one outlined in Chapter 1 (the Potter Box Model) assist in developing and revising a strategy?*

C H A P T E R   S U M M A R Y

This chapter has outlined that a great number of protests take place every year and the majority of those pass peacefully with police officers being equipped in only their regular uniform and communicating with the protestors in a peaceful and friendly manner. It is only when protests turn violent or protestors engage in criminality that emphasis on maintaining control rather than enforcing the law becomes paramount (Waddington, 2007). The debate about how to ensure that police behave with integrity and ethically within these situations has been articulated in a series of reports by the HMIC (2009a, 2009b and 2011). Given the confrontational nature of violent protests, where a significant amount of violence and aggression is directly aimed at the police themselves, ethical strategies and tactics that take into consideration human rights, proportionality and accountability are being developed and implemented. The use of ethical decision-making models can not only assist in the development of the strategies, but can also offer a tool when commanders have to change tactics as the nature of protests changes in real time. In July 2011, ACPO published a Statement of Mission and Values, which makes specific reference to when police officers are confronted with violence:

> *In the face of violence we will be professional, calm and restrained and will apply only that force which is necessary to accomplish our lawful duty. Our commitment is to deliver a service that we and those we serve can be proud of and which keeps our communities safe.*

(ACPO, 2011)

FURTHER READING

The chapter draws upon a number of key texts from the subject area. However, a number of reports on policing public order by the HMIC are essential reading. These include *Keeping the Peace: Policing disorder* (1999), *Adapting to Protest* (2009), *Adapting to Protest: Nurturing the British model* (2009) and *Policing Public Order* (2011). In addition, PAJ Waddington's writings on public order are considered the seminal academic reference on this subject matter.

REFERENCES

ACPO (Association of Chief Police Officers) (2011) *Statement of Mission and Values.* Presented at the Higher Education Forum for Police Learning and Development, University of Northampton, 6 September.

Grieve, J, Harfield, C and MacVean, A (2007) *Policing: Sage course companion.* London: Sage.

History House (2011) The Last Reading of the Riot Act on Mainland UK. Online at www.historyhouse.co.uk/articles/riot_act.html (accessed 24 November 2011).

HMIC (Her Majesty's Inspectorate of Constabulary) (2009a) *Adapting to Protest.* London: HMSO.

HMIC (Her Majesty's Inspectorate of Constabulary) (2009b) *Adapting to Protest: Nurturing the British Model.* London: HMSO.

HMIC (Her Majesty's Inspectorate of Constabulary) (2011) *Policing Public Order.* London: HMSO.

Hutton, G and McKinnon, G (2008) *Blackstone's Police Manual.* Oxford: Oxford University Press.

Inquest (2011) Jury's Verdict of Unlawful Killing at Inquest into Death of Ian Tomlinson Vindicates Family and Public Concern. Online at http://inquest.gn.apc.org/website/press-releases/press-releases-2011/verdict-unlawful-killing-ian-tomlinson (accessed 24 November 2011).

Jefferson, T (1990) *The Case Against Paramilitary Policing.* Maidenhead: Open University Press.

Jerrard, R (2003) Breach of the Peace. Internet Law Book Reviews. Online at www.rjerrard.co.uk/law/cases/bibby.htm (accessed 24 November 2011).

Mark,R (1978) *In the Office of Constable.* London: Collins.

Ministry of Justice (2011) Statistical Bulletin on the Public Disorder of 6th to 9th August 2011. London: Ministry of Justice. Online at www.justice.gov.uk/downloads/publications/statistics-and-data/mojstats/august-public-disorder-stats-bulletin.pdf (accessed 24 November 2011).

Open University (2009) Police and Public Order. Online at www.open.ac.uk/Arts/history-from-police-archives/Met6Kt/PublicOrder/poHvyHnd.html (accessed 22 November 2011).

Reiner, R (1985) The Politics of the Police. London: Harvester Wheatsheaf.

Roger,C, Lewis, R, John, T and Read, T (2011) *Police Work (Principles and Practice).* London: Routledge.

Sanders, A and Young, R (2003) Police Powers, in Newburn, T (ed.) *Handbook of Policing.* Cullompton: Willan.

Townshend, C (1993) *Making the Peace: Public order and public security in modern Britain*. Oxford: Oxford University Press.

Waddington, PAJ (1998) Both Arms of the Law: Institutionalised protest and the policing of public order, in *Papers from the British Criminology Society Conference*, Loughborough University, 18–21 July 1995. Online at www.britsoccrim.org/volume1/008.pdf (accessed 3 December 2011).

Waddington, PAJ (2003) Policing Public Order and Political Contention, in Newburn, T (ed.) *Handbook of Policing*. Cullompton: Willan.

Waddington, PAJ (2007) Policing of Public Order. *Policing: A Journal of Policy and Practice*, 1(4): 375–7.

Waddington, PAJ (2008) Public Order, in Newburn, T and Neyroud, P (eds) *Dictionary of Policing*. Cullompton: Willan.

USEFUL WEBSITES

www.hmic.gov.uk – Her Majesty's Inspectorate of Constabulary

www.homeoffice.gov.uk – Home Office

www.legislation.gov.uk – most types of legislation, including the Human Rights Act 1998

8 Ethical considerations in covert investigations

CHAPTER OBJECTIVES

By the end of this chapter you should be able to:

- understand how ethics are considered in covert policing;
- recognise the different types of covert policing and ethical risks;
- understand the debates and challenges of applying an ethical framework to covert practice;
- identify the legislation that regulates and guides covert strategy and practice;
- appreciate the ethical risks and dilemmas when considering covert policing.

LINKS TO STANDARDS

This chapter provides opportunities for links with the following Skills for Justice, National Occupational Standards (NOS) for Policing and Law Enforcement 2008.

AE1.1   Maintain and develop your own knowledge, skills and competence.
CA1   Use law enforcement actions in a fair and justified way.
HA1   Manage your own resources.
HA2   Manage your own resources and professional development.
POL1A1 Use police action in a fair and justified way.

With the introduction of the Qualification and Credit Framework (QCF), it is likely that the term 'National Occupational Standards' will change. At the time of writing it is not clear what the new title will be, although it is known that some organisations will use the term 'QCF assessment units'.

Links to current NOS are provided at the start of each chapter; however, it should be noted that these are currently subject to review and it is recommended that you visit the Skills for Justice website to check the currency of all the NOS provided: www.skillsforjustice-nosfinder.com.

Introduction

Billingsley (2001) has estimated that almost one third of all crimes solved by the police involve the use of police informers and covert police activity. However, the involvement of police informers and covert police methods is higher in more serious crime. That is because, generally, criminals remain clandestine about their activities so as not to be apprehended by the police and punished for their law breaking. Criminality often involves deceit, dishonesty and duplicity, and criminals frequently associate with other criminals to facilitate and assist in law breaking and to prevent detection. It is often difficult for the police to obtain information and evidence of such criminal activity unless they engage in similar behaviour. Yet this means that the police have to inhabit a world working alongside known offenders, dealing with deception, lies and betrayal, or using covert methods of policing, which invade people's privacy and interfere with individual rights to family life. Integrity and truth are masked behind relationships and strategies based on betrayal, duplicity and intrusion. This raises the question of whether such police tactics can be subjected to ethical practice. In order to begin to understand how ethical and value-based principles can be understood and applied to covert policing, the necessity for such police techniques needs to be examined.

There has been a shift in policing directives since the 1990s, leading to an increase in intelligence-led policing, bringing with it greater proactive policing initiatives and covert activity (Neyroud and Beckley, 2001b). As serious and organised crime, mainly focused around drug trafficking, became a significant issue in the 1970s and 1980s, it was recognised that reactive policing (which was generally the response to a victim statement or crime scene) was not effective in policing crimes that were organised, sophisticated or involved several criminals. Therefore, reactive policing was replaced by proactive strategies, involving the gathering of information and intelligence by infiltrating the criminal fraternity (Kruisbergen et al., 2011).

This change in policing methods altered the terms of the debate from regarding covert policing as simply a form of state intrusion and the advancement of the 'big brother' society towards a recognition of the need to engage a wide variety of policing methods (overt and covert) in order to fight and combat crime. In particular, the debate began to focus not so much on the use of undercover policing or the developing technology to assist covert operations, but on managing and controlling the use of covert activity with the necessary degree of proportionality and accountability (Garland, 1995; Marx, 1988; Neyroud and Beckley, 2001a).

This debate raises a number of complex and difficult questions in relation to the ethics of covert police work.

- Should the police engage in similar deceptive practices as criminals?

- To what extent should the police engage in such practices?

- Can covert policing achieve its objectives, namely to bring criminals to court?

- Can deceptive practices by the police be ethical and follow a set of principle values?

- How can covert police activity be regulated and managed effectively so that unethical practice is avoided?

- How should covert policing be protected within the power of the law?

This chapter examines the various types of covert techniques and how these particular tactics pose ethical risks and dilemmas. It outlines the guidelines, policies and legislation covering covert policing, ensuring that deception and intrusion into privacy are account-able, justified and proportional and that there is a system of ethical responsibility.

REFLECTIVE TASK

- *Is the use of covert policing necessary to tackle crime in England and Wales?*

- *Is it ethical for police to deploy deceptive and duplicitous tactics in the fight against crime?*

Covert investigative methods

There are a number of different covert methods that the police use to investigate crime. These fall into three broad categories: surveillance, the use of informers, which is known as the management of covert human intelligence sources (CHIS), and the accessing and interception of communication. All methods are offender-focused, involve deception and intrude into the privacy of individuals, thus potentially compromising their human rights.

Surveillance

Surveillance is defined as the monitoring of behaviour and activities, normally of offenders or those suspected of committing or about to commit a crime, often by secret and clan-destine methods. It can involve technologies such as CCTV or the use of human agents. Ericson and Haggerty (1997) argued that surveillance is a key aspect of policing, as police routinely gather information on criminals to develop problem-oriented and intelligence-led strategies to combat and prevent crime. Surveillance uses a range of covert techniques, including the undercover tracking of offenders and suspects.

Informers, or covert human intelligence sources

Police informants, or covert human intelligence sources (CHIS), are often criminals who provide the police with information about other criminals or criminal activities for a reward. These rewards include money, reduction in charges or sentence, or some other form of favour. It has been argued that police informers pose the greatest risk to the integrity of policing and are involved in many cases of police corruption (Billingsley et al., 2001). The Audit Commission (1993) concluded that some police forces were disinclined to use informers because of the ethical problems they presented. There is the principle that criminals should not be rewarded for their knowledge or association with criminal activity. There is also a view that, if the police engage with 'dirty and tainted' criminals, it can in turn taint and corrupt police work (South, 2001). The chapter later discusses some of the ethical and moral issues when using informers.

Accessing and intercepting communication

The police can gather information and intelligence by intercepting communication devices such as telephones and other forms of equipment. However, this information cannot be used as evidence in a British court of law. Justice, the organisation for advancing justice, human rights and the rule of law, has forcefully argued for the use of intercepted communication as evidence in court: *The UK is the only country in the common law world that prohibits completely the use of intercepted communications as evidence in criminal proceedings* (Justice, 2006).

They argue that the government's ban on not using intercepted material in court is archaic, unnecessary and counterproductive in the fight against terrorism and crime.

CASE STUDY

Every year, about 1,500 intercept warrants are issued to enable the police and intelligence agencies to listen to the conversations of suspects believed to be involved in serious criminality. Yet, under the Regulation of Investigatory Powers Act 2000, none of the evidence obtained by this covert method of policing is allowed to be used in any part of the prosecution process. While telephone interception evidence is not admissible in court, neither can the question be asked of whether any telephones were intercepted during the course of the police investigation. However, any conversation recorded on a hidden microphone or covert filming during the investigation is admissible in court.

In the following scenario, the police were investigating an operation that involved smuggling drugs into the UK. An intercept warrant had been approved and the relevant intercept mechanisms were put into place. During the course of the operation, the information received from the interception indicated that the criminals also had links to a terrorist organisation. From the intercepted telephone recordings, the police identified that the terrorist organisation was going to plant a bomb in a night club on a particular Saturday night. This enabled the police to prevent the terrorists from carrying out their actions while still allowing the interception to continue in relation to the importation of drugs.

REFLECTIVE TASK

- *Do you believe that intercept evidence should be used as evidence in a court of law?*

- *What are the potential issues for police in relation to ethics and accountability if intercept evidence were to become admissible as evidence in court for both terrorist activity and the importation of drugs?*

- *What are the ethical arguments for not allowing intercept evidence to be admissible in court?*

In each of the covert methods discussed above, Neyroud and Beckley (2001a) identify two areas of concern for policing: deception and intrusion into privacy.

Deception

The intention of police officers to deceive deliberately by lying raises the question as to whether it is morally wrong, or whether there is a case for it being morally permissible, or indeed whether there is a moral obligation for police officers to engage in covert activity. Marx (1988) attempts of answer this moral dilemma by stating that deception can be considered in two distinct forms, either as 'ethical deception' or 'deceptive ethics'.

Marx (1988) regarded ethical deception as something that required careful consideration. He suggested that you need to assess the proportionality of the actions by understanding the intended and unintended outcomes of the deception. Only then could you assess whether the deception could be justified. In explaining covert policing, he argued that both social contract theory and Utilitarianism endorsed the use of such methods, providing the assessment was justified, as society had invested in the police to use such methods if it was for good and greater ends (Neyroud and Beckley, 2001a).

However, deceptive ethics rejects the use of methods that involve lying and deceit, particularly in the name of the state, and therefore any covert methods for police investigation are simply unacceptable.

These two forms of deception raise more moral questions than provide answers. Although they provide an academic framework in which to situate deception, they do not provide a framework for what is acceptable and what is not in deploying deceptive police activity.

Intrusion into privacy

Surveillance, CHIS and accessing and intercepting communication represent a significant intrusion into a person's privacy. Article 8 of the Human Rights Act 1998 (HRA) clearly sets out the right to respect for private and family life, but this right is qualified with certain restrictions that are 'in accordance with the law' and 'necessary in a democratic society', as stated below.

Article 8, Human Rights Act 1998

1. *Everyone has the right to respect for his private and family life, his home and his correspondence.*

2. *There shall be no interference by a public authority with the exercise of this right except such as is in accordance with the law and is necessary in a democratic society in the interests of national security, public safety or the economic well-being of the country, for the prevention of disorder or crime, for the protection of health or morals, or for the protection of the rights and freedoms of others.*
   (www.legislation.gov.uk/ukpga/1998/42/schedule/1)

While human rights principles provide a framework for what is acceptable in relation to intrusion into a person's privacy by considering the conflicting rights of the victim, the suspect and society, there is the element of ethical decision making when police officers have to interpret and deal with situations as they arise during undercover operations. In the wider debate about routine collection of personal data by the state, Chesterman (2011) argues that society should not be concerned about intrusion into our privacy by the routine collection of information about us by governments and agencies as, in this globalised context, this is inevitable; rather, society should be more concerned about how these agencies use the information. This is a new social contract in which society should expect a degree of intrusion into privacy in order that government may provide security for the nation.

Ethical considerations for covert policing

Can covert policing ever be ethical? It is easy to recognise what is unethical practice; this can be explained by non-compliance with legislation, failing to meet professional standards and engaging in corrupt behaviour. Williamson and Bagshaw (2001, quoting Cooper and Murphy (1997)), give an example of informant handlers as a cost-effective way of preventing and detecting crime:

> *Figures from Merseyside from April 1994 to February 1995 show that by paying informers £55,000 they recovered £0.8 million in stolen property, £0.75 million in drugs 13 firearms, achieved 450 arrests and one murder conviction.*
>
> (Williamson and Bagshaw, 2001, p55–6)

However, generally, the financial costs attributed to using informers often fail to include any expenses occurred while managing them and include only the cost paid out to them. So, while there is an argument as to whether covert policing is cost-effective, so too is there an ethical one. To justify covert policing, Williamson and Bagshaw (2001) provide a 'fourfold route to justification' as follows.

1. *Deception is essential to achieve this particular task.*

2. *The achievement of this task is essential to carry out the role.*

3. *The role is essential to the effectiveness of the police service.*

4. *The police service is necessary and justified and therefore the deception is necessary and justified.*

(Williamson and Bagshaw, 2001, p56)

While this fourfold route may justify the need for covert investigation, there needs to be a closer examination of the ethics of the decision-making process when considering whether to employ covert policing tactics.

It is helpful to adapt some of the nine points of Rushworth Kidder's ethical decision-making model in relation to making ethical decisions for covert policing.

Kidder's ethical decision-making model

1. Recognise that there is a moral/ethical issue.

2. Whose issue is it?
   a. Is it a police responsibility?
   b. Are the police morally obligated to do anything?

3. Gather the relevant facts.
   a. What events have unfolded?
   b. What else might happen?
   c. Who may have or is withholding information?
   d. What is the future potential?

4. Test for right-versus-wrong issues.
   a. What covert policing options do I have?

5. Test for right-versus-right paradigms. What sort of dilemma is this?
   a. Is it a case of truth versus loyalty?
   b. Is it a case of self versus community?
   c. Is it a case of short-term versus long-term?
   d. Is it a case of justice versus mercy?

6. Apply the resolution principles.
   a. *Ends-based thinking*: Do what's best for the greatest number of people.
   b. *Rule-based thinking*: Follow your highest sense of principle.

7. Investigate the 'trilemma' options.
   a. Is there a third way through this dilemma?

8. Make the decision.

9. Revisit and reflect on the decision.

   (Adapted from Kidder, 1995; www.cs.bgsu.edu/maner/heuristics/1995kidder.htm)

While the Kidder model has been adapted, it does nonetheless provide a model for how covert policing techniques can be ethically considered.

REFLECTIVE TASK

There has been a series of burglaries in a suburban area of Newtown. These burglaries occur shortly after the postman has finished completing his rounds in the area. The postman returns to the depot and spends several hours preparing work for the following day.

It is suspected that the postman checks to see if anyone is at home in a particular property and telephones his associate to inform him that a particular house is empty.

REFLECTIVE TASK continued

- *Going through each point of Kidder's ethical decision-making model, consider whether it is morally proportionate and justified to intercept the postman's mobile telephone calls/conversations?*

Another model to consider for covert investigations is the PLAN concept. PLAN provides a value-based approach through considering the following.

P – Proportionality

What type of covert method is proportionate to obtain the information or intelligence being obtained?

L – Legitimacy

What is the legitimate purpose of the proposed action (prevention or detection of crime, interests of country, the protection of rights and freedoms of others etc)?

A – Authority to undertake the proposed action

What is the lawful basis and authority for the proposed action? Has the necessary authority been obtained?

N – Necessity of proposed action

Why is the proposed action necessary?

(Adapted from Harfield and Harfield, 2005)

Integrity and the ethical risks of being an undercover police officer

There are a number of ethical risks involved for police officers who are involved in covert policing as well as those who authorise covert investigations. Deceptive practice by its very nature compromises integrity.

This was highlighted in an HMIC report, *Police Integrity: Securing and maintaining public confidence* (1999):

> *In the context of a potential lack of integrity, the use of informants is possibly the highest-risk area in the work of the modern Police Service . . . There is nothing new about using informants but it was suggested to the Inspection Team that their use caused so much controversy and difficulty for the Service and individual handlers with limited benefit, it should be stopped altogether. It is, however, a fact many people involved in law enforcement believe informants are valuable and necessary. Her Majesty's Inspectorate agrees providing informants are properly targeted and controlled . . .* **Her Majesty's Inspectorate is extremely concerned to discover that effective systems for ensuring informants are used with integrity either do not exist at all or are ignored.**

(HMIC, 1999, p23; our emphasis)

However, it is important to note that, since 1999, significant advances have been made to ensure that regulation and effective systems are now in place to ensure greater integrity. Nonetheless, there is always an element of risk in relation to corruption while the police seek to engage informers as partners in crime prevention, as shown in the case study below.

CASE STUDY

John Donald and Kevin Cressey

In 1992, two notorious criminals, Kevin Cressey and David Fraser, were arrested by the Regional Crime Squad for possessing a large amount of cannabis and a loaded firearm. Immediately following his arrest and understanding the predicament he was in, which involved a potential long prison sentence, Cressey set about corrupting a police officer. During the hours following his arrest, Cressey indicated to police officers that he held valuable information and was willing to become a police informer. While in police custody, several police officers attempted to recruit Cressey as an informer without success, until Detective Constable John Donald tried. Cressey saw something in Donald that he could corrupt and became registered as a police informer with Donald as the informant handler.

This allowed Cressey and Donald to meet legitimately and have regular contact with each other. The first act of corruption was when Cressey offered to pay £40,000 to Donald to remove the evidence that centred upon his original arrest for possessing drugs and a loaded firearm. Donald's attempt to steal this evidence was prevented by an honest police officer.

However, what is remarkable in this case is that the role of informer and informant handler quickly became reversed. Instead of Cressey providing information to the police, Donald provided Cressey with secret police intelligence relating to other criminals and forthcoming police operations. It is believed that Cressey sold this information on to other criminals. However, Cressey still had to stand trial for the crimes he was originally arrested for and would have faced a lengthy period of imprisonment. In an attempt to damage the reputation of the police investigation and in particular Donald, Cressey approached a television company and informed them of his relationship with Donald. The television company secretly recorded, over the following weeks, several meetings between Cressey and Donald and the programme was screened in September 1993. Subsequently, both Donald and Cressey were arrested and, at the ensuing trial, Donald was sentenced to 11 years' imprisonment and Cressey to seven years.

REFLECTIVE TASK

- *Could a set of ethical guidelines have prevented the corruption of the police officer as described in the above case?*

- *Is there a case where it is moral and ethical to pay criminals for information about crime and other criminals?*

REFLECTIVE TASK *continued*

- *What guidelines could be established to prevent such corrupt practices?*

- *Is there a justifiable case for the rare occasions when police corruption occurs for the greater good of covert policing?*

Legislation and guidelines regulating covert activity

Legislation and guidelines are the most formal mechanisms to control and ensure that covert tactics are ethically considered and deployed. However, as Kruisbergen et al. observed: *The ideology of policing by consent was accompanied by a common law tradition of implicit police powers, namely police activity required no explicit legal authorisation* (2011, p394)

However, the first break with this tradition was the Police and Criminal Evidence Act 1984, which regulates stop and search, arrest and detention. In part, this provides guidance as to what is acceptable police activity, balancing the competing rights of the offender and those on whose behalf the police act. There are three main pieces of legislation concerned with covert police activity: the Human Rights Act 1998, the Police and Criminal Evidence Act 1984 and the Regulation of Investigatory Powers Act 2000.

The Human Rights Act 1998

It is important to clarify the relationship between human rights law and covert police activity. The Human Rights Act 1998 (HRA) provides a mechanism for members of the public to seek redress in UK courts if public authorities, including the police, fail to comply with the European Convention on Human Rights (ECHR). The ECHR places clear obligations on the police to ensure that their actions are lawful, necessary and proportionate (Grieve et al., 2007). The overriding objective of the HRA is to ensure that the police do the right things in the right way for the right reasons (Grieve et al., 2007).

In relation to article 8 of the HRA, it is important to note that the article is not a right to *privacy and a private life*, but a right to *respect* for private and family life. Therefore, this right is a qualified and not an absolute right and, provided there is legal provision to do so, its protections may be breached in certain circumstances, such as intrusive surveillance to assist in detecting and preventing serious crime. While a country cannot derogate from absolute rights, qualified rights may be breached if domestic law gives provision, such as the Regulation of Investigatory Powers Act 2000, the Police and Criminal Evidence Act 1984 and other laws giving police specific powers. This protection to the individual is afforded through international instruments, domestic law and case law, including the HRA. In the absence of a code of ethics for the police in England and Wales, these provide a framework to ensure that the police conduct covert operations ethically and through a clearly defined legal framework.

The Police and Criminal Evidence Act 1984

The Police and Criminal Evidence Act 1984 (PACE) began to regulate rules of exclusion for evidence obtained through covert methods. Section 78 of the Act stated that courts may refuse to allow evidence should it have an adverse effect on the fairness of the trial proceedings because of the method by which it was obtained. This clause was created as a result of concerns about confessions that had been obtained under duress and evidence from 'supergrasses' or criminal informers that may have been given as a result of inducements. The fabrication of confessions, known as 'verballing', was criticised by both the public and the courts as corrupt police practice that needed to be challenged and regulated. Where a suspect had 'confessed', it was often difficult for the police to prove that the confession had been voluntary. These concerns led to a Royal Commission on Criminal Procedure in 1981, which directed a set of reforms to regulate the arrest, detention and questioning of suspects. PACE also sought to control information obtained from informers by making it inadmissible in court: *deception in criminal investigation could be considered acceptable up to the doors of the interview room and no further and, above all, not in the trial process* (Skolnick, 1967, quoted in Billingsley et al., 2001, p164).

So, while PACE regulated and controlled the information obtained by informers in the trial process by demanding greater disclosure of information, including monetary rewards to those providing information to the police, it did not provide for any regulatory framework for the police working with informers.

Regulation of Investigatory Powers Act 2000

Prior to the Regulation of Investigatory Powers Act 2000 (RIPA) was the Interception of Communications Act 1985. It is important to understand how the latter Act came into being and how it was repealed and replaced by RIPA.

The judgment of the European Court of Human Rights in *Malone v. United Kingdom* (1985) led directly to the enactment of the Interception of Communications Act.

CASE STUDY

Malone *v.* United Kingdom *(1985)*

James Malone resided in Surrey and, in 1977, was charged with handling stolen goods. He was acquitted of this charge but, during the trial, it emerged that his telephone conversations had been intercepted on a warrant issued on the authority of the Home Secretary. Malone issued civil proceedings in the High Court against the Metropolitan Police Commissioner, claiming that interception of his telephone was unlawful even if it had been executed under a warrant signed by the Home Secretary. This claim was dismissed. In 1979, Malone took the case to the European Commission of Human Rights and, in 1984, the Commission stated that there had been a clear breach of his rights under article 8 of the ECHR, namely the right to respect for private and family life.

This European directive led to the enactment of the Interception of Communications Act 1985, which meant that telephone interception could not be used as admissible evidence in court.

However, the Interception of Communications Act was repealed by schedule 1 of RIPA and replaced by part 1 of RIPA.

RIPA regulates all public bodies, including the police, when carrying out surveillance and investigation. For the first time, RIPA provided a statutory framework for the police in an area that had previously been regulated only by case law. RIPA also ensures that any covert activity is compliant with the HRA while empowering law enforcement agencies to deal with advancing technology increasingly used by criminals. Jack Straw stated that RIPA:

> *merely formalised existing powers. Covert surveillance by police and other law enforcement officers is as old as policing itself. What is new is that for the first time the use of these techniques will be properly regulated by law.*

(BBC, 2000)

The Act has also been subject to substantial further amendments in subsequent legislation (Harfield and Harfield, 2005).

While RIPA provided a statutory framework for covert policing, it has been criticised for giving greater emphasis to managerial and administrative processes rather than providing ethical guidance and values.

REFLECTIVE TASK

John Brown is a known petty criminal engaging in some drug dealing and opportunistic burglary. Intelligence has reported that he has been seen several times with prominent criminals who are suspected of stealing high-value cars and trading in firearms to gangs. It is suspected that Brown is becoming a key associate of these criminals and that they are planning and organising a significant firearms deal.

In order to gather more information, the police consider instigating a covert operation.

- *Are there relevant and sufficient grounds based on reliable information for conducting a covert investigation and, in particular, what specific covert methods should be considered?*

- *Could the same information or intelligence be gained by less intrusive methods?*

- *Can the covert investigation be accountable, proportional and justified in all aspects of the investigation?*

- *Is the balance of protecting society and individual rights proportional and just?*

- *Is the operation compatible with the European Convention on Human Rights?*

C H A P T E R   S U M M A R Y

This chapter has explored ethical considerations in relation to covert investigations. It has examined the tensions of covert policing, namely the need to gain information otherwise not available to the police to prevent and detect crime while respecting the intrusion into the private lives of individuals.

The increasing use of legislation to regulate and control covert activities has shown that, while it provides some administrative guidance for the police to ensure that they do not act unfairly or unlawfully, it offers very little ethical advice.

While covert policing is a 'necessary evil', much of the information or evidence gleaned is deemed to be inadmissible in a court of law. Further, the process of covert policing involving deception and duplicity poses potential risks for police officers to become corrupted. However, there are concepts, such as PLAN and Kidder's ethical decision-making model, that are based upon ethical principles and value systems that can support a greater ethical approach when considering covert strategies.

FURTHER READING

Much of the reading in this chapter is drawn from a range of academic books, statutes and policy documents. However, *Informers: Policing, policy and practice* by Billingsley et al.(2001) and *Covert Investigation* by Harfield and Harfield (2005) provide a comprehensive overview of the ethical and legal challenges in covert policing in relation to both use of police informers and operational good practice.

REFERENCES

Audit Commission (1993) *Helping With Enquiries.* Police Paper No. 12. London: HMSO.

BBC (2000) Surveillance Bill under Fire. BBC News, 10 February. Online at http://news.bbc.co.uk/1/hi/sci/tech/638041.stm (accessed 24 November 2011).

Billingsley, R, Nemitz, T and Bean, P (eds) (2001) *Informers: Policing, Policy, Practice.* Cullompton: Willan.

Chesterman, S (2011) *One Nation Under Surveillance: A new social contract to defend freedom without sacrificing liberty.* Oxford: Oxford University Press.

Cooper, P and Murphy, J (1997) Ethical Approaches for Police Officers when Working with Informants in the Development of Criminal Intelligence in the UK. *Journal of Social Policy,* 26(1): 1–20.

Ericson, RV and Haggerty, KD (1997) *Policing the Risk Society.* Oxford: Oxford University Press.

Garland, D (1995) Panopticon Days: Surveillance and society. *Criminal Justice Matters,* 20(1): 3–4.

Grieve, J, Harfield, C and MacVean, A (2007) *Policing: Sage course companion.* London: Sage.

Harfield, C and Harfield, K (2005) *Covert Investigation.* Oxford: Oxford University Press.

HMIC (Her Majesty's Inspectorate of Constabulary) (1999) *Police Integrity: Securing and maintaining public confidence.* London: HMSO.

Justice (2006) Intercept Evidence: Lifting the ban. Online at www.justice.org.uk/resources/php/40/intercept-evidence (accessed 24 November 2011).

Kidder, RM (1995) *How Good People Make Tough Choices.* New York: William Morrow.

Kruisbergen, E, Jong, D and Kleesmans, E (2011) Undercover Policing: Assumptions and empirical evidence. *British Journal of Criminology*, 51: 394–412.

Marx, G (1988) *Undercover: Police surveillance in America.* Berkeley, CA: University of California Press.

Neyroud, P and Beckley, A (2001a) *Policing, Ethics and Human Rights.* Cullompton: Willan.

Neyroud, P and Beckley, A (2001b) Regulating Informers, in Billingsley, R, Nemitz, T and Bean, P (eds) *Informers: Policing, Policy, Practice.* Cullompton: Willan.

Skolnick, J (1967) *Justice Without Trial.* New York: Wiley.

South, N (2001) Informers, Agents and Accountability, in Billingsley, R, Nemitz, T and Bean, P (eds) *Informers: Policing, Policy, Practice.* Cullompton: Willan.

Williamson, T and Bagshaw, P (2001) The Ethics of Informer Handling, in Billingsley, R, Nemitz, T and Bean, P (eds) *Informers: Policing, Policy, Practice.* Cullompton: Willan.

USEFUL WEBSITES

www.legislation.gov.uk/ukpga/1998/42/schedule/1 – Human Rights Act 1998, schedule 1

9 Police corruption and misconduct

Introduction

There has been a history of police misconduct and malpractice since the inception of the modern police force. Kleinig argues that:

Corruption in police work has been a pervasive and continuing problem. Almost every serious history of policing and even of particular police departments has had to confront the issue of police corruptibility.

(Kleinig, 1996, p163)

This view of police corruption is also endorsed by Newburn (1999), who stated that corrupt practices are found in many police agencies in some form or another throughout most societies. In addition, Newburn argues that corruption occurs in all ranks, not merely within the lower ranks, and there are certain sectors of policing that are more at risk of corruption than others. Punch concluded that corruption is found in all countries, in all forces and at every level of the organisation at some time, indeed *policing and corruption go hand in hand* (2009, p1). However, what is not known is the nature and extent of corrupt activities that occur at any one time in a department, force or nationally. As we will see in this chapter, police corruption can be taken to include a wide variety of problems that range from 'noble cause' corruption, to financial and personal gain, and to the abuse of authority and position as a police officer.

Police corruption and deviance are viewed as particularly abhorrent as the police are meant to enforce the law impartially and with integrity; the legitimacy of policing by consent is founded on the very principles of impartiality and integrity (Sherman, 1978).

Yet, as Punch (2009) posits, police officers are faced with an impossible dilemma by the very role of policing; police officers are expected to perform the task of upholding the law in a framework of legislation, limited resources and intricate rules that restrict how they can go about their job (Maurice, 2009). Manning (1977) refers to this as the 'impossible mandate' that *fosters diverse forms and patterns of deviance and corruption which are related to achieving formally approved goals or covert, illicit ends* (quoted in Punch, 2009, p2).

Despite the acceptance that policing and corruption 'go hand in hand', most police officers are neither deviant nor corrupt. This poses a number of ethical questions.

- What makes a police officer corrupt and engage in criminal behaviour?

- How does corrupt and deviant behaviour manifest itself between police officers?

- Do police officers view deviant behaviour as corrupt, or as necessary practice in fulfilling their role?

- How can corrupt behaviour be defined for the purposes of ethical police practice?

- Does the police organisation itself encourage corrupt behaviour and practice?

- Why is it that some police officers do not engage in corrupt activity?

- Does a 'blue code of silence' exist between corrupt and non-corrupt police officers?

- How can ethics assist in recognising, challenging and dealing with corrupt behaviour?

This chapter considers why corruption and misconduct harm the police in their ability to fulfil their functions, how an ethical framework can assist in understanding deviant behaviour and how such behaviour can become manifest within the police environment and what can be done to address it.

REFLECTIVE TASK

- *List the different types of deviant police activities that can be classified as corruption.*

- *Are some types of corrupt behaviour more serious than others? Explain your answer.*

- *Why does the nature of police work make it more vulnerable to corrupt practices?*

- *How do you think a professional code of ethics would help in understanding the nature and form of deviant behaviour?*

Defining police corruption and misconduct

Police corruption and deviant behaviour encompass a wide range of activities and interactions between different groups of people. Kleinig (1996) argues that it is the very nature of police work that makes it particularly vulnerable to deviant behaviour. He provides four reasons for this vulnerability.

1. One of the fundamental roles of policing is to apprehend those who break the law. Some criminals have a vested interest in preventing the police from carrying out this role effectively and are aware of the considerable discretion that police officers have and that they may be able to be influenced by bribery and other forms of illegality. Some police officers may be tempted to accept these bribes and inducements in return for not effectively enforcing the law against these criminals.

2. Corruption can also be encouraged by the wider community, who want a greater policing presence and entice officers to spend more time in a particular area or establishment by inducing them with incentives such as free services or meals. This is often referred to as the corruption of authority.

3. One of the elements of police culture is cynicism, and the day-to-day contact with law breakers creates a moral cynicism in which not only criminals but all citizens are seen to be corrupt and corrupting. Corruption therefore becomes something that everyone is engaged in, and it may be viewed by some officers as a reward for being a police officer and having the responsibility of dealing with the unpleasant side of human behaviour.

4. The police themselves are often unwilling to admit that police corruption exists within their department or force. This unwillingness to acknowledge that police corruption exists has made the reporting of corrupt practices difficult and thus only recently have there been reliable systems and structures in place to deal with police deviancy. Historically, police corruption has often been exposed by the media or by a public inquiry. It was not until Sir Robert Mark, the Commissioner of the Metropolitan Police

Service from 1972 to 1977, publicly pledged to rid Scotland Yard of corrupt police officers, that endemic police corruption was acknowledged by the police service itself.

Notwithstanding that the police service may be more vulnerable to corrupt practice by the very nature of its function, corruption is notoriously difficult to define. The term 'corruption' is used to describe a range of illicit police behaviours, from falsifying evidence, to obtaining personal gains for either pursuing or not pursuing an investigation, accepting bribes for not reporting criminal activity, partaking in criminal activity, providing police information to criminals, opportunistic thefts and corruption of authority. Corrupt behaviour can occur within the police organisation as well as without. The HMIC report, *Police Integrity: Securing and maintaining public confidence* (1999), identified a link between misconduct and unacceptable behaviour tolerated within the police organisation and corrupt practice: *In an environment where bullying, arrogance, rudeness, racist or sexist behaviour is tolerated, corruption and other wrongdoing will flourish, and is more likely to remain unreported* (HMIC,1999, p9).

The complex and elusive nature of corrupt behaviour often means that corruption is defined either by particular cases or by broad typologies of deviant behaviour, but what all actions of deviant behaviour or misconduct have in common is that they are inextricably linked to abuse of official power, abuse of position and abuse of trust (Punch, 2009; Newburn, 1999).

There are several models for the various typologies of corrupt activity; however, one of the most often quoted is that put forward by Roebuck and Barker (1974). They identify eight different categories, with Punch adding a ninth class (see Table 9.1).

While typologies of corrupt activities are useful, there also needs to be a definition for corruption. There have been several attempts to provide an overarching definition for corruption and malpractice, ranging from a broad notion of corruption to more, quite specific, definitions. For example, Roebuck and Barker (1974) define corruption as: *deviant, dishonest, improper, unethical or criminal behaviour by a police officer*. Goldstein (1977) offers a similar definition: *the misuse of authority by a police officer in a manner designed to produce personal gain for the officer or for others*.

Other definitions are often more specific, referring to a particular type of corrupt activity:

> *James Q Wilson (1968), for example, distinguishes between activities such as accepting bribes (which he considers to be the prototypical form of corrupt behaviour) and 'criminal' activities such as burglary on duty (which he considers to be qualitatively different – criminal but not corrupt). Although both acts are criminal, the point of Wilson's distinction is that bribery of police officers involves the exploitation of authority in a way that burglary by police officers need not.*
>
> (Newburn, 1999, p5)

Other definitions proposed have included specific activities that define corruption. McMullan's definition states:

> *a public official is corrupt if he accepts money or money's worth for doing something he is under a duty to do anyway, that he is under a duty not to do, or to exercise a legitimate discretion for improper reasons.*
>
> (1961, p183)

Table 9.1 Typology of corrupt activities

Category of corrupt activity	Characteristics
Corruption of authority	This is where police officers receive some material benefit or financial gain merely because of their position as police officers, for example, free drinks, meals or other services.
Kickbacks	This is where police officers receive material benefits and financial gain through the recommendation of business to particular individuals or companies.
Opportunistic thefts	This is where police officers steal when an opportunity is presented to them, such as stealing from an arrestee, traffic accident victim or crime victim, or taking the property of dead citizens.
Shakedowns	A shakedown is the acceptance of a bribe for not following through a criminal charge as the police officer would otherwise do. This could include not making an arrest or recording a complaint.
Protection of illegal activities	This is where police officers will afford protection to those engaged in illegal activities, enabling the business to continue, such as drugs, prostitution, money laundering etc.
Fixing	Fixing involves the disruption and intercepting of criminal investigations or proceedings, such as through removing files or losing paperwork.
Direct criminal activities	This is where police officers commit direct criminal violations against a person or property for their own personal gain or benefit.
Internal payoffs	This is where police officers sell their own internal advantages to other officers, including holidays, shift allocations and even promotions to other departments/teams.
Planting or padding evidence	This is where police officers plant or add evidence in a particular case. One of the most common forms of this is the planting of drugs at a scene of crime or on a person who is about to be or has been arrested.

Punch (1985) provides a more sophisticated definition:

> *when an official receives or is promised significant advantage or reward (personal, group or organizational) for doing something that he is under a duty to do anyway, that he is under a duty not to do, for exercising a legitimate discretion for improper reasons, and for employing illegal means to achieve approved gaols.*
>
> (quoted in Newburn, 1999, p6)

Punch's definition acknowledges that corrupt behaviour may be not only for personal gain but also for the gain of a wider group of people (either a police or criminal group) or for the benefit of the wider police organisation (Newburn, 1999).

However, the definitions above do not readily encompass deviant behaviour that is illegitimate or unacceptable but that does not involve personal, group or organisational gain, such as drug taking, sleeping while on duty, consuming alcohol while on duty, reckless driving and so on. This type of activity has been referred to as 'misconduct' and the difference between corruption and misconduct is that misconduct does not involve personal gain and, as such, the 'motivation' for securing personal profit is not present.

This presents an ethical dilemma: is misconduct a form of corrupt and deviant behaviour? Consider the following case studies.

CASE STUDIES

Case study 1
A police department responsible for tackling and responding to drug crime in a city has a significantly high success rate and has been identified as an area of good practice. However, unbeknown to management, the reason for the success rate is that a number of police officers within the department plant drugs on suspects who they know deal in drugs but about whom they do not have enough evidence to ensure a conviction. This enables the department to ensure that the cases they investigate tend to result in positive convictions.

Case study 2
In a training department, a member of staff sends a homophobic email to another colleague within the department. This colleague challenges the behaviour of the member of staff who sent the email. In the ensuing management investigation, the member of staff who sent the email colluded with another colleague in the department to state that while the homophobic image was constructed on the computer, it was never distributed, but only shown to colleagues, and therefore the member of staff who complained about receiving the email must have accessed her colleague's computer when she was away from the desk and sent it to her own computer.

REFLECTIVE TASK

- *Does one of the cases above involve more 'corruption' or deviant behaviour than the other, making it therefore more serious than the other?*

- *Should the sanctions of the deviant police officers in both cases be the same or should officers in one of the cases be treated more leniently, and why?*

- *Does the behaviour of the police officers in both cases show any common patterns?*

- *What are the implications for those who report corrupt behaviour and misconduct?*

Kleinig (1996) has put forward a more general definition of corruption, in that he considers the orthodox theories of corruption and extends this to include what has also been described by other academics as 'misconduct': *police officers act corruptly when, in exercising or failing to exercise their authority, they act with the primary intention of furthering private or departmental/divisional advantage* (Kleinig, 1996, p166).

Kleinig himself states that his definition is 'very radical' in that it covers many acts and practices that may not normally be perceived as corrupt, such as pursuing one criminal case more actively than another as it would bring the officer more standing and enhance his or her professional reputation. Thus, the officer is duty bound to pursue both cases equally and fairly, but chooses not to, purely for personal advancement. Kleinig argues that *such practices are motivated by the 'spirit' of corruption, and belong to the same moral category as corruption that is more visibly deleterious* (1996, p166). Therefore, motivation for behaviour is a critical factor in determining what defines corrupt activity, rather than focusing on types of activity in isolation. According to Kleinig (1996), if motivation is a key factor in deviant behaviour, corruption becomes an ethical rather than a legal or administrative problem. It only becomes a legal or administrative problem in that this is how the deviant behaviour is often presented and addressed by the organisation. Therefore, deviant activity itself is not corrupt; it is the *desire* for some form of gain, being financial or non-financial and for personal, group or organisational benefit, that is the corrupting factor.

REFLECTIVE TASK

Reflecting upon Kleinig's theory that police deviant behaviour is primarily an ethical problem rather than a legal or administrative one, consider the case studies above and review your responses to the questions in the previous reflective task.

- *Would you change any of your responses to the four questions?*

- *Have you now considered the means, the ends and the motivation behind the deviant behaviour?*

Newburn (1999) makes five general observations in trying to define and understand police corruption.

1. *In attempting to define corruption, attention must be paid to the means, the ends and the motivation behind the conduct.*

2. *Corruption need not necessarily involve illegal conduct or misconduct on the part of a police officer (the goals of the action may be approved).*

3. *Corrupt acts may involve the use **or** the abuse of organisational authority.*

4. *Corruption may be 'internal' as well as 'external', i.e. it may simply involve two (or more) police officers.*

5. *The motivation behind an act is corrupt when the primary intention is to further private or organisational advantage.*

(Newburn, 1999, p8)

CASE STUDY

In 1996, West Yorkshire police investigated the murder of Joe Smales, aged 85, and an attack on his brother, Bert, who was 68 years old. The key prosecution witness in this case was Karl Chapman, who was a jailed supergrass and £100,000 had been set aside by West Yorkshire Police for Chapman upon his release from prison in exchange for providing 'evidence' against the two main suspects, Paul Maxwell and Daniel Mansell. However, during the period of obtaining evidence from Chapman, it was alleged that detectives allowed him to visit a brothel, take class A drugs in front of them and have sex with a female officer in exchange for giving evidence against Maxwell and Mansell. Maxwell and Mansell's conviction was quashed in 2009 as a result of the tainted and corrupt investigation.

A Supreme Court ruling in August 2011 revealed the shocking and appalling misconduct of police as they conspired to pervert the course of justice at the trial of Maxwell and Mansell. The court heard that vast amounts of documents, tapes and other information vital to the case had been destroyed, some after West Yorkshire Police had been given official notice to preserve such evidence. The Supreme Court ruling said the high-ranking officers from the force conspired together to pervert the course of justice and that their behaviour was 'shocking and disgraceful'.

Maxwell's barrister, Patrick O'Connor, said:

One of the most striking aspects of the saga is the extent to which this many officers, and these senior officers, seemed to have behaved with apparent impunity between them.

They seemed to act as if they had no fear that one of their colleagues was going to inform on them and bring their conduct to a halt. They trusted each other implicitly didn't they?

An investigating officer from an outside force trying to investigate the scale of the conspiracy said some of the officers were results-driven and not very concerned with procedures. He added:

With regard to senior officers, it is clear that there could be more professional auditing, tasking and checking but there wasn't. That culture seemed to permeate throughout the inquiry.

REFLECTIVE TASK

- Can using definitions and typologies of corruption assist in understanding the nature and extent of corrupt behaviour?

- How can Kleinig's ethical model of motivation assist in explaining why the police officers became involved in deviant behaviour in the above case?

- What lessons can be learnt from this case in recognising when corrupt practice occurs, and what structures and systems could be established to prevent this behaviour from occurring again?

Good community policing or corrupt practice?

One of the long-standing debates in the ethics of corruption is whether gratuities constitute deviant behaviour or are in fact part of good community policing. The police officer who regularly patrols a beat area may be frequently offered a cup of tea or sandwich by the local café. The newsagent may give the officer a box of chocolates as a Christmas present. The public house may offer him or her a free drink after work. Is this the blurred boundary of corrupt practice or is it being a good community police officer?

Police managers attempting to address corruption may take a hard-line approach and insist that the acceptance of even a 'free cup of tea' offered on the beat by local cafés would be treated as corrupt behaviour. Yet, the ethos of community policing is for officers to be able to effectively know, converse with and understand all the communities that they police. So while, on the face of it, this dilemma seems to be an administrative issue, Kleinig (1996) argues that, in fact, it is an ethical one. Kleinig distinguishes the differences between gratuities and bribes, in that bribes generally have a significant value and are often in proportion to the deviant behaviour expected in return. In addition, a bribe is offered and accepted in order to corrupt authority, to influence the behaviour of the police officer in a way that is negative to their responsibilities.

> *A gratuity, on the other hand, is often just a token, a gesture of appreciation. When police managers talk about gratuities, they tend to have in mind free cups of coffee and doughnuts no less than larger gifts.*

(Kleinig, 1996, p171)

However, Jones and Newburn (1998) contest that the acceptance of gratuities goes against the democratic principles of policing and that some members of the community offering such gratuities disadvantages those who do not offer gratuities. By accepting gratuities, the police presence is unfairly distributed to the area where the gratuities are offered (Feldberg, 1985). Kleinig (1996) goes some way to support this argument; if the gratuities are made on a regular and systematic basis, it may create a sense of obligation and also suggests that this may be the first stage on the 'slippery slope' of corrupt practice.

Newburn provides a useful summary of the ethical advantages and disadvantages of accepting gratuities (see Table 9.2).

There is no right or wrong answer to whether gratuities construct or facilitate corrupt behaviour, but the debate highlights the complexity of misconduct and that an ethical framework is far more beneficial in understanding the issues than an administrative or legal model. However, as mentioned at the beginning of the chapter, police corruption is a pervasive and continuing problem and it is useful to understand why it continues to flourish despite numerous attempts to eradicate it. One of the reasons attributed to the continual endurance of police deviancy is the secrecy fostered by police peer groups.

Secrecy within and throughout the police ranks

McConville and Shepherd (1992) have stated that one of the most important lessons that student officers learn in their first year is not to discuss or talk about practices they have

Table 9.2 Advantages and disadvantages of accepting gratuities

Advantages		Disadvantages	
Appreciation	It is natural for members of the community to show their appreciation to those providing a public service.	Sense of obligation	Even the smallest gift inevitably creates a sense of obligation if it becomes regularised.
Not significant	The gratuities are not significant enough to buy or cultivate favour.	Slippery slope	Gratuities lead to a 'slippery slope' where the temptations become imperceptibly greater and refusal increasingly difficult.
Officially offered	When gratuities are offered by a company or corporation, no personal sense of obligation can develop.	Remove temptation	Not all officers can exercise proper judgement on what is reasonable to accept. It is more sensible for the organisation to remove temptation altogether.
Community links	The ethos of community policing is to forge links with the community. This can include accepting and sharing a 'cup of tea'.	Purchase preferential treatment	Businesses that offer gratuities are, in essence, seeking to purchase preferential treatment (e.g. encourage greater police presence in the vicinity of their business).
Police culture	Accepting gratuities is an entrenched part of police culture. Any attempt to end it would result in displeasure and cynicism by both police officers and some members of the community.		
Trust and discretion	Attempts to prevent acceptance imply that officers cannot be trusted to exercise discretion and are incapable of making sensible moral judgements to guide their behaviour.		

Source: Newburn (1999, p10).

witnessed by their experienced colleagues, including those breaching the rules in order to discharge their policing duties. This secrecy becomes part of the police culture and one that bonds police officers and police departments. This bond of secrecy forms part of the set of informal rules and norms that inform and organise police groups and departments. Sherman (1978) states that these informal rules and norms serve two purposes: first, to minimise external control over the department and, second, to ensure that corrupt activities are maintained at a level that can be managed and controlled internally within the department. This code of silence is often referred to as the 'blue code of silence' (Skolnick, 2002) or the 'blue curtain of secrecy' (Sherman, 1978). Alongside the code of silence are strong bonds of loyalty that develop between groups and departments. This loyalty has also been identified as both facilitating and encouraging corrupt behaviour. In addition, it also frustrates enquiries and control mechanisms. Newburn (1999) highlighted how these codes of secrecy and strong bonds were acknowledged in the Wood Commission, which was a commission set up to investigate endemic levels of corruption, graft and vice in New South Wales, Australia, in 1997. The Wood Commission (1997) concluded:

> *The strength of the code of silence was evident during the Commission hearings. Almost without exception officers approached by the Commission initially denied ever witnessing or engaging in any form of corrupt activity. Even with an undertaking that police would not be disciplined for failing to report certain forms of corruption, the offer of amnesty and the availability of protection against self-incrimination, officer after officer maintained this stand until presented with irrefutable evidence to the contrary. Each knew the truth, yet the strength of the code, and the blind hope that no one would break it, prevailed.*

(quoted in Newburn, 1999, p155)

The Wood Commission identified four key reasons as to how the code of silence contributes to the emergence of corruption.

- A code of silence influences honest and inexperienced officers to accept corruption as part of the job.

- For managers, this code of silence was so endemic that it ensured that corruption could not be challenged, nor could the police service be reformed.

- The code of silence also enabled corrupt police officers to manipulate and control fellow officers.

- The code of silence also actively frustrated any inquiry into corruption.

The Wood Commission also concluded that the code of silence permeated all ranks of the police service and was not confined to just the 'rank and file'. This widespread approach to the code of silence encourages the police to adopt an adversarial position to anyone who is not a police officer, anyone who challenges police activity and those police officers who do not engage in adopting a 'code of silence' stance (Wood, 1997).

REFLECTIVE TASK

You are part of a police team that is deployed every Friday and Saturday evening to patrol High Grange town. The town has numerous pubs and two nightclubs, and the team deals with the normal level of anti-social behaviour and criminality on those two nights that is comparable to other similar towns. You patrol the street with two other officers. You become aware that, in order to increase their number of arrests, the other two officers 'goad and encourage' drunken youths, who are being no more than slightly loud, to be

REFLECTIVE TASK *continued*

aggressive towards them. This has involved one officer slapping youths across their faces in order to provoke a reaction. In another case, one of the officers held one youth while the other officer took money from the youth's wallet.

You are appalled and distressed by your colleagues' behaviour.

- *What options can you consider in trying to address your colleagues' behaviour?*

- *What moral and ethical dilemmas are involved in each of your options above?*

- *Are your options based on your personal commitment to integrity, or your sense of loyalty to your colleagues, or a combination of both?*

- *Did you consider the 'code of silence' as one of your options?*

- *Did you feel that you would be considered a 'grass' if one of your options was to report your colleagues' behaviour to a superior?*

Kleinig (1996) identifies nine broad options that an officer could consider in the above case study.

1. Join in the unethical conduct.

2. Turn a blind eye to it.

3. Seek to dissuade those involved.

4. Ask for a transfer to another shift or department.

5. Report the behaviour to your superior.

6. Make the deviant behaviour public by reporting it to an outside agency or the media.

7. Resign (and then make the deviant behaviour public). If implicated, then 8 or 9 below.

8. Tough it out.

9. Cooperate with the investigating team.

REFLECTIVE TASK

What are the advantages and disadvantages of Kleinig's nine options stated above?

New and emerging forms of corruption

If corruption is a pervasive and continuing problem, there is an assumption that deviant behaviour can never be eradicated but only controlled. New forms of technology and communication provide new methods that can assist and facilitate corrupt practice. In 2010, The Serious Organised Crime Agency (SOCA) undertook an assessment of the current scale of corruption within the British police after senior officers raised serious concerns about the increasing number of allegations of corruption being brought to their attention. In particular, three new areas have been identified where officers of all ranks can be exploited by criminals or those with an interest in ensuring the police do not carry out their role effectively. First, social networking sites are where police officers often identify themselves as working for the police service and are therefore open to approaches from the criminal fraternity. Second, there is increasing use of and access to confidential information on police IT systems; information is obtained and exchanged by police officers for either inappropriate personal use or for financial gain. Third, at gyms police officers can be known to take steroids, leading them into contact with criminals (Lavell, 2010).

These new areas allowing for corruption mean that the police remain as vulnerable today to being targeted by criminals as they were in the 1970s, when police corruption was thought to be at its height. Corruption today has been identified in many different forms of deviant behaviour and includes police officers spending public money for their own use, having sex with vulnerable women who have been arrested, blackmailing people on police databases, tipping off criminals about current police operations or passing along information on rival criminals, stealing property and passing confidential information to criminals. In addition to increasing forms and levels of police corruption, there is also evidence to suggest that criminal gangs are placing their own associates into the police service as police officers both to provide information and to recruit corrupt police officers into their criminal activities.

These new and emerging forms of police corruption require greater vigilance by police managers, as well as a greater emphasis for all police officers on ethics and integrity if they are to be confronted and challenged (Neyroud and Beckley, 2001; Kleinig, 1996)

C H A P T E R   S U M M A R Y

This chapter has considered the relationship between policing and corrupt behaviour, and how ethics and integrity can help in understanding how deviant behaviour manifests itself in both individual police officers and police departments. It has examined the challenges of defining police corruption and identified typologies of corrupt practices. This chapter has highlighted that, while the nature and extent of corruption remains elusive, it is accepted that it is a pervasive and continuing problem that occurs at all levels of the police organisation.

The chapter explored the difficulty of how corruption and misconduct was not always clear-cut, giving the example of how gratuities could be seen as either corrupt practice or good community policing. It further identified how the 'blue code of silence' can assist and facilitate corruption and misconduct and, finally, how new methods of communication and IT can encourage new forms of corruption. Throughout the chapter, it was acknowledged that deviant behaviour could never be eradicated, but suggested that an ethical framework could help police officers identify corrupt behaviour and respond to it effectively.

There is a wide range of books and articles on police corruption but, for the purposes of providing a comprehensive overview of ethics and integrity in relation to deviant behavious, *The Ethics of Policing* by Kleinig (1996), *Policing, Ethics and Human Rights* by Neyroud and Beckley (2001), *Police Corruption: Deviance, accountability and reform in policing* by Punch (2009) and *Understanding and Preventing Police Corruption: Lessons from the literature* by Newburn (1999) all provide excellent accounts.

Feldberg, M (1985) *Gratuities, Corruption and the Democratic Ethos of Policing: The case of the free cup of coffee*, in Elliston,F and Feldberg,M (eds) *Moral Issues in Police Work*.Totowa, NJ: Rowman and Allanheld.

Goldstein, H (1977) *Policing a Free Society.* Cambridge, MA: Ballinger.

Jones, T and Newburn, T (1998) *Private Security and Public Policing.* Oxford: Clarendon.

Kleinig, J (1996) *The Ethics of Policing.* Cambridge: Cambridge University Press.

HMIC (Her Majesty's Inspectorate of Constabulary) (1999) *Police Integrity: Securing and maintaining public confidence.* London: HMSO.

Lavell, S (2010) Serious Organised Crime Agency Turns Spotlight on Police Corruption. *The Guardian*, 14 February.

Manning, PK (1977) *Police Work.* Cambridge, MA: MIT Press.

McConville, M and Shepherd, D (1992) *Watching Police, Watching Communities*. London: Routledge.

McMullan, M (1961) A Theory of Corruption. *Sociological Review*, 9: 183–94.

Newburn, T (1999) *Understanding and Preventing Police Corruption: Lessons from the literature.* London: Home Office.

Neyroud, P and Beckley, A (2001) *Policing, Ethics and Human Rights*. Cullompton: Willan.

Punch, M (2009) *Police Corruption: Deviance, accountability and reform in policing*. Cullompton: Willan.

Roebuck, J and Barker, T (1974) *An Empirical Typology of Police Corruption.* Springfield, IL: Thomas.

Sherman, L (1978) *Scandal and Reform: Controlling police corruption.* Berkeley, CA: University of California Press.

Skolnick, J (2002) Corruption and the Blue Code of Silence. *Police Practice and Research*, 3(1): 8.

Wilson, JQ (1968) *Varieties of Police Behaviour.* Cambridge, MA: Harvard University Press.

Wood, JRT (1997) *Final Report of the Royal Commission into the New South Wales Police Service.* Sydney: RCNSWO.

www.acpo.gov.uk – Association of Chief Police Officers

www.homeoffice.gov.uk – Home Office

www.soca.gov.uk – Serious Organised Crime Agency

10 Professional standards and ethical practice

CHAPTER OBJECTIVES

By the end of this chapter you should be able to:

- understand the context of professional standards in relation to ethics and values;
- recognise the structure and remit of professional standards departments and organisations;
- understand how misconduct is constructed and dealt with both internally and externally, providing independence and accountability;
- identify the ethical principles that underpin the disciplinary process;
- reflect on how learning from complaints can provide a more ethical approach to operational policing.

LINKS TO STANDARDS

This chapter provides opportunities for links with the following Skills for Justice, National Occupational Standards (NOS) for Policing and Law Enforcement 2008.

AE1.1	Maintain and develop your own knowledge, skills and competence.
CA1	Use law enforcement actions in a fair and justified way.
HA1	Manage your own resources.
HA2	Manage your own resources and professional development.
POL4C1	Develop one's own knowledge and practice.

With the introduction of the Qualification and Credit Framework (QCF), it is likely that the term 'National Occupational Standards' will change. At the time of writing it is not clear what the new title will be, although it is known that some organisations will use the term 'QCF assessment units'.

Links to current NOS are provided at the start of each chapter; however, it should be noted that these are currently subject to review and it is recommended that you visit the Skills for Justice website to check the currency of all the NOS provided: www.skillsforjustice-nosfinder.com.

Introduction

The report *Police Integrity* (HMIC, 1999) highlighted that there can be *no more important qualities for members of the Police service than that they are honest and act with integrity* (1999, p1). This report further articulated that police integrity encompassed more than just the narrow dimension of corruption, which had eroded public confidence during the 1970s and 1980s, and included issues such as fairness, probity, decent behaviour and equal treatment. It highlighted that the police's primary role was upholding and administrating the law fairly and without prejudice. The public expected the highest standards of professional behaviour of the police, not least because of the considerable power and authority invested in them by the state. While Neyroud and Beckley (2001) have argued that it is complex to recognise what a principled police service looks like, it is easy to identify unprincipled, unethical and bad behaviour. However, once bad behaviour and misconduct by police officers are identified, it is essential to understand how the police organisation responds to and deals with them and how much of the process is governed within an ethical and principled approach. This chapter will examine professional standards through the codes that define what is acceptable and what is unacceptable behaviour and the procedures in place to deal with police discipline.

In 2006, the then Home Secretary, Hazel Blears, announced that there was to be a new Code of Professional Standards for the police service. The outdated Code of Conduct was to be replaced by a new police disciplinary system that focused on the concepts of equality, accountability and professionalism. This new Code of Professional Standards had been informed by the Taylor Review (2005). The Taylor Review argued that an effective, accountable police service that commands public confidence required a more professional approach and that, significantly, every police officer needs to have a clear understanding of the high standards of conduct expected from them. The Taylor Review emphasised that management of misconduct issues should not just be about imposing punishment and sanctions, but developing a culture of learning for the individual and organisation so that future behaviour is improved.

This new approach to professional standards would allow the connections between agency and structure to be explored, and expose the intricate and complex relationships between ethics, morality, culture, politics and myths in relation to unethical and bad behaviour.

REFLECTIVE TASK

- *What do you understand by the term 'professional standards'?*
- *How can an understanding of ethics inform professional standards?*

Professional standards

Chapter 2, 'Professional policing and a code of ethics', provided an understanding of what a profession was and whether the police service was considered to be a profession.

Therefore, it follows that professional standards refer to the standards of practice of the police as they carry out their policing tasks. These standards of practice encompass more than the perfunctory duties of the police, and include other consequential acts such as confidentiality, deception, consent and coercion (Hughes, 2011). Therefore, the ethical and principled practice of carrying out tasks is also a consideration of profession standards. As Hughes states: *This is reflected in the way we talk about 'higher' and 'lower' standards, and implicitly appeals to another, normative, standard – that is, a standard of how police ought to behave* (2011, p14).

Therefore, as Hughes (2011) further suggests, professional standards, either in a descriptive or normative sense, need not exist in written form, but are considerations of how the police conduct themselves or how they ought to conduct themselves. Many professional organisations do have written forms of professional standards, often referred to as codes, statements or declarations, which formally set out rules and guidelines that outline the responsibilities and expected standards of conduct and practice for individuals and the organisation.

Professional standards differ greatly in their structure and form for each profession:

> *Some affirm broad principles or values of an overtly moral nature while others are much more specific and practical. Some set out strict rules backed with disciplinary sanctions, while others provide guidance and advice. Some propose minimum standards below which members of the profession must not fall while others set inspirational ideals. These approaches may be combined, either within a single document or in a set of related publications.*
>
> (Hughes, 2011, pp14–15)

Thus, professional standards set out the values and conduct of the behaviour that is expected from members of a profession. However, this raises the question, while professional standards may promote and ensure that behaviours are maintained to a specific standard, do they necessarily advance ethical and integral practice and, if so, can this be applied in the context of policing? It has to be remembered that police officers are not 'employees' in the traditional sense but 'servants of the Crown' and this position enhances their independence by avoiding the conventional employment arrangements enjoyed by other public servants or the private sector. This means that police officers are not subject to the normal sanctions of employment law. This unique position is further enhanced by the police officer status of 'office of constable', whereby officers have operational independence empowered with extraordinary legal powers and are answerable to the law alone (Taylor, 2011). Thus, it follows that any professional standards mechanism will be different from those of other professions and will have specific challenges.

In relation to professional standards and policing, two broad aspects are particularly relevant to police ethics and values. The first is that the selection and recruitment process should be suitable to ensure that recruits with the right traits and characteristics for police officers are taken on, and that these positive values are enhanced and developed throughout the training process. The second is that the term 'professional standards' refers to the process and practice of investigating complaints made against police officers, including investigations where police corruption and malpractice are suspected. These two issues are examined in turn.

Professional standards in the selection and recruitment process of police officers

Neyroud and Beckley (2001) argue that establishing ethical behaviour and practice in police officers should commence with the selection and recruitment process. It is easy to identify what characteristics are not desirable or required in a police officer, but it is more difficult to establish the values and ethics of a police recruit.

PRACTICAL TASK

- *Make a list of the skills, abilities and values that would not be desirable for someone considering becoming a police officer.*

- *Make a list of the skills, abilities and values that are desirable for someone considering becoming a police officer.*

- *Consider how you can ascertain the values that a person may hold in the recruit selection process.*

There are a number of processes in police recruitment that are designed to ascertain the skills, abilities and values of people applying to become police officers. These include the National Police Selection Process, which includes role plays, one-on-one interviews, various written examinations and a fitness test, in order to assess numerical and logical reasoning skills, speed and accuracy skills, and verbal and written abilities, as well as how physically fit recruits are. In addition, extensive medical and security checks are undertaken. While this seems a comprehensive and detailed selection process, Neyroud and Beckley (2001) suggest that it may overlook the ethical traits of a recruit. Using research undertaken by Covey (1989), they argue that there are two distinct models of ethical characteristics that dominate recruitment processes. The first is referred to as the 'personality ethic' and the second as the 'character ethic'. Covey's research established that, in the last 50 years, the 'personality ethic' has become dominant as the criterion for success. Prior to that, success had been achieved by the 'character ethic'. Of relevance to police recruitment are the attributes of each ethic type: the personality ethic has attributes of superficiality, image consciousness, skills, techniques and quick fixes through human and public relations techniques and positive mental attitudes; whereas the character ethic features integrity, humility, fidelity, temperance, courage, justice, patience, industry, simplicity and modesty. Therefore, as Neyroud and Beckley (2001) propose, the recruitment process should include an element to test for the character ethic of an applicant. In addition, they further advocate that the selection procedure should recognise emotional intelligence (EI) in potential recruits, which takes into account reason and intuition, as opposed to the standard IQ (intelligence quotient) tests. They support their argument through the research conducted by Goleman (1996), who states that, at best, IQ only contributes

20 per cent to the factors of life success. Therefore, by introducing selection criteria that measure the character ethic as opposed to the personality ethic, and EI rather than IQ, the police service may recruit a more ethical police officer (Neyroud and Beckley, 2001).

In 2000, the report of the Rampart Inquiry was published. The Rampart Inquiry was an investigation into the corrupt activities of the Community Resources Against Street Hoodlums (CRASH) unit of the Los Angeles Police Department. The report concluded that more than 70 police officers were involved in misconduct, many of a serious nature, making it one of the most widespread cases of police misconduct in the USA. Twenty-four of these police officers were convicted for a range of offences, including stealing drugs, fabricating evidence, engaging in unprovoked shootings, committing bank robberies, planting guns on unarmed suspects, severely beating suspects in custody and intimidating witnesses. As a result of the investigation into falsified evidence and perjury, 106 criminal convictions were overturned. In addition, over 140 civil lawsuits were brought against the police, costing more than 125 million dollars in settlements.

The Rampart Inquiry exposed that the corruption was endemic throughout the department, including the supervisors, who were implicated in holding celebrations and rituals to celebrate and reward the corrupt behaviour.

Punch (2010) states that police deviance elicits various forms of harm and creates diverse victims (p78). Victims included members of the public who were injured, shot at, wounded and even killed, as well as people who were set up for crimes that they did not commit.

For Neyroud and Beckley (2001), the significant issues from the Rampart Inquiry focused on police values and integrity. They highlighted that many of the officers allowed their personal integrity to erode and their activities certainly had a contagious effect on other staff (p170).

Neyroud and Beckley further highlighted the Inquiry categories of recommendations, which included:

- *testing and screening of police officer candidates;*
- *personnel practices;*
- *corruption investigations;*
- *ethics and integrity training;*
- *anti-corruption inspections and audits.*

Policing professional standards

Up until 1977, police forces themselves were responsible for investigating complaints of police misconduct and corruption that occurred in their force area, although the Home

Secretary had the power to refer serious allegations to another force for investigation. This internal management of complaints, with a lack of perceived independence, attracted strong criticisms following a series of corruption scandals in the mid-1970s. This criticism led to the creation of the Police Complaints Board in 1977, which was tasked with overseeing complaints made against police officers or police forces. The Board was empowered under the Police (Complaints) Act 1976 to review and scrutinise reports produced by an investigating force in order to satisfy themselves that the investigation had been fair, accountable and just. It could further instruct the Chief Constable of the force to pursue disciplinary action against offending police officers. However, it has been argued that the Police Complaints Board was ineffective and, while there was general disquiet about its role, the procedure it adopted became controversial when a case resulted in double jeopardy against a police officer who had earlier been exonerated by the Director of Prosecutions. The Scarman Report (1981), following the Brixton Riots, was also critical of the Police Complaints Board and there was pressure to reform it. The result was that the Board was abolished and replaced by the Police Complaints Authority (PCA) in 1985. The PCA was given greater powers, allowing it to supervise police investigations into complaints, although it was not empowered with its own independent investigatory powers. The PCA was subsequently replaced by the Independent Police Complaints Commission (IPCC) in 2004.

While the IPCC investigates serious complaints and oversees the system of Professional Standards within police forces, all police forces have their own Professional Standards Department. Both the IPCC and Professional Standards Departments are discussed in more detail later in the chapter. It is, however, important to remember that the majority of complaints of misconduct to Professional Standards Departments arise from internal concerns rather than members of the public.

REFLECTIVE TASK

The Macpherson Report (1999) on the death of Stephen Lawrence stated:

> The need to re-establish trust between minority ethnic communities and the police is paramount . . . seeking to achieve trust and confidence through a demonstration of fairness will not in itself be sufficient. It must be accompanied by a vigorous pursuit of openness and accountability.

- *Consider how operational autonomy of the police and an external oversight with its own investigatory power yet totally free from the influence of the police are necessary and essential to ensure that the public have and maintain confidence in the police.*

- *How can these two organisations exist side by side to ensure that the police service operates ethically and is accountable for its actions?*

The Taylor Review

Against the backdrop of increasingly independent oversight through the PCA and the IPCC, there was a desire to reassess how misconduct should be dealt with at local force level, given that the majority of complaints came from within the organisation. In 2004, the then Home Secretary commissioned a review on the current arrangements for dealing with police misconduct and unsatisfactory performance. This review was to look into the effectiveness of the disciplinary arrangements for police officers.

Up until this review, the police disciplinary process mirrored the militaristic and legalistic approach that had dominated the modern police force (Taylor, 2011). For a significant period of time, disciplinary rules and regulations focused on what police officers were prohibited from doing, creating a negative approach to dealing with unacceptable and corrupt behaviour. The driver for the Taylor Review can be traced back to 1999, when a philosophical shift from a 'disciplinary code' to a 'code of conduct' took place. The issue of a police code of ethics had been discussed for several years following the creation of a police ethics working party in 1992 to consider and develop a code of ethics to make policing more principled (Boggan, 1992). Although a code of ethics was not adopted nationally by police forces, the Police Service of Northern Ireland (PSNI), formed from the Royal Ulster Constabulary in 2001, did adopt a code of ethics.

The terms of reference for the Taylor Review was to consider police disciplinary arrangements and the extent to which they provide a proportionate, just and effective process for the disposal of conduct and complaint matters; and in a way that is likely to enjoy the confidence of the public and the police (Taylor, 2005).

In addition, the remit sought to consider the extent to which the Code of Conduct is fit for purpose and the potential for the development and possible incorporation of a code of ethics, demonstrating that the aspiration for a code of ethics for the police service to be incorporated into professional standards was still very much on the political agenda.

The Taylor Review reported that the system for dealing with police misconduct was bureaucratic and legalistic with little incentive for managers to deal swiftly and proportionately with low-level misconduct cases. These cases were heard by a panel of three senior police officers. Disciplinary cases were also adversarial in context and not conducive to either individual or organisational learning. The review made six key recommendations.

Key recommendations of the Taylor Review

1. A new single code (incorporating ethics and conduct) should be produced to be a touchstone for individual behaviour and a clear indication of organisational and peer expectations.

2. Disciplinary arrangements should be established on the basis of 13 key factors, including:
   - a culture of learning;
   - appropriate language and environment;
   - formal assessment of initial complaints;
   - two categories of misconduct and gross misconduct;

- misconduct should be dealt with at the lowest level of management;
- investigations should be proportionate and less formal;
- a simple appeals process;
- disciplinary arrangements must be dynamic;
- independent oversight agencies must be robust in challenging poor practice;
- time limits must be set and adhered to;
- poor performance should not be inappropriately managed as poor behaviour.

3. A working group should be established to present to the Police Advisory Board.

4. A review of the Unsatisfactory Performance Procedures should be undertaken.

5. The review of the disciplinary procedures for police staff should be published as soon as possible.

6. If the Taylor Review recommendations are adopted, the issues of 'taint and disclosures' should be reassessed.

(Adapted from Taylor, 2005)

The Taylor Review signalled a radical new approach to police discipline and misconduct. It heralded a shift from blame and sanction to development and improvement. It further ensured that only matters relating to misconduct were reviewed under the new form; matters relating to capability and performance should be dealt with as a separate issue. Public complaints were to remain citizen-focused but were not to be complainant-driven, and proportionality was the key element that had to be applied to all parties.

The government adopted the recommendations made in the Taylor Review and subsequently implemented them through the Police (Conduct) Regulations 2008, which provided new misconduct procedures for all police officers.

Police (Conduct) Regulations 2008

The Police (Conduct) Regulations 2008 provide the statutory framework for dealing with allegations of misconduct among police officers. The Regulations detail the procedures that have to be followed on matters relating to police discipline. The procedure is established on an initial full assessment of the alleged misconduct at an early stage and with a view to implementing a proportionate and non-legalistic or bureaucratic response.

The Regulations reflect the procedures followed in employment contexts outside the police service and, more specifically, remove the disciplinary sanctions of a requirement to resign, reduction in rank, reduction in rate of pay, fine, reprimand and caution. These disciplinary sanctions are replaced with management action, written warning and final warning. The Regulations define conduct as being either misconduct or gross misconduct. Misconduct is considered as a breach of the Standards of Professional Behaviour, with gross misconduct being a serious breach that may justify dismissal.

The emphasis of the new arrangements was to resolve disciplinary proceedings swiftly. This was a significant departure from the previous position. Significantly, the disciplinary proceedings are meant to consider whether a police officer has breached the standards expected. The standard of proof in such cases is the civil standard, primarily the balance of probabilities. The public interest lies in action being taken against the officer where possible, rather than the officer being suspended on full pay awaiting a potential criminal trial.

REFLECTIVE TASK

- *Consider how the philosophical shift in the disciplinary process from blame and sanction to one of development and learning has impacted on the public perception of the police in relation to corruption and misconduct.*

- *Think about how previous forms of sanction – requirement to resign, demotion of rank, reduction in the rate of pay and fines – may have contributed towards a culture where misconduct and unethical practice could flourish.*

Professional Standards Departments

Since 2000, most police forces in England and Wales have significantly expanded the departments that deal with police misconduct, complaints and discipline. These units are now generically referred to as Professional Standards Departments (PSDs). The increasing concern of the police service about police misconduct highlighted in the HMIC report, *Police Integrity: Securing and maintaining public confidence* (1999), engendered a number of recommendations to improve integrity, which led to the PSDs adopting a more proactive response to police misconduct and corruption.

PSDs have an operational team (or teams), supported by an intelligence cell that manages a central database where information is gathered and analysed. This information comes from a variety of sources, including members of the public, criminal informants, police officers, other agencies, audits or checks on internal information systems and surveillance intercept (Miller, 2003).

PSDs also investigate the misconduct and unethical behaviour of police staff and special constables. Research shows that the PSDs tend to deal with cases of misconduct that are broadly divided into two organisational forms: individual corruption or, less commonly, internally networked forms of corruption. Individual corruption involves police officers or members of staff engaging in corrupt activities, generally in isolation from their colleagues. Internally networked corruption involves the more traditional view of corruption, implicating detectives in the CID or specialist units. This form of corruption normally involves corrupt relationships between police officers and informants (Miller, 2003).

The PSDs have four key functions (HMIC, 2006).

- To know the health of professional standards within the police force.

- To improve and prevent the abuse of professional standards.

- To ensure that they are effective at dealing with emerging professional standards issues.

- To have the capacity and capability to address reactive and proactive challenges.

Independent Police Complaints Commission

The IPCC became operational on 1 April 2004. It has a legal duty to oversee the whole of the police complaints system, created by the Police Reform Act 2002. Its aim is to transform the way in which complaints against the police are handled. One of the drivers for the development of the IPCC was the lack of confidence in the independence of police complaints, which was highlighted in the Macpherson Report (1999). The concept of an independent oversight agency with its own investigatory powers has been mooted for several years. Both the Scarman Report (1981) and the Macpherson Report (1999) called for such a body. As Macpherson stated:

> [It is recommended t]hat the Home Secretary, taking into account the strong expression of public perception in this regard, consider what steps can and should be taken to ensure that serious complaints against police officers are independently investigated. Investigation of police officers by their own or another Police Service is widely regarded as unjust, and does not inspire public confidence.
>
> (Macpherson, 1999, recommendation 58)

The Commission's overall purpose under the Police Reform Act is twofold:

- to ensure suitable arrangements are in place for dealing with complaints or allegations of misconduct against any person serving with the police;

- in doing so, to increase public confidence by demonstrating the independence, accountability and integrity of the complaints system and so contribute to the effectiveness of the police service as a whole.

The IPCC maintains its independence by ensuring that the Chair or any of the Commissioners for the IPCC have not previously worked for the police service in any capacity.

Complaints are directed to the IPCC either directly from the public or from police forces. Many of the complaints received directly from the public are not serious enough to warrant a full investigation and are generally, with the consent of the complainant, passed back to the local police force concerned to be dealt with by their PSD. The IPCC received around 15,000 such complaints during 2009–10. Those complaints that warrant investigation will be allocated either 'independent' or 'managed or supervised' investigation status. Independent investigations are carried out by the IPCC and managed or supervised investigations are carried out by the local force under the control and supervision of the IPCC. In addition, the IPCC has a duty to investigate the most serious cases involving death or serious injury through police conduct, police misconduct involving serious assault, sexual assault, corruption, criminal offence or discriminatory behaviour, and fatal force and deaths in custody (Jackson, 2011).

However, alongside this, the IPCC has become the pivotal organisation to capture the learning from complaints and disseminate this back to forces. This has enabled forces nationally not only to learn from complaints, but to consider the learning within an ethical and value framework, allowing them to develop ethical practice.

PRACTICAL TASK

- *Go to the IPCC website at www.ipcc.gov.uk. Access the IPCC Resource tab and open up the Research and Statistics file. Open up the* Public Confidence in the Complaints System Survey.

- *Read through the survey and consider if the IPCC has increased public confidence in the police through independent oversight of police complaints.*

- *Browse the IPCC website to establish how it disseminates the learning from complaints back to police forces. A good report illustrating this learning ethos is the one on the Deaths in Police Custody Study (December 2010). Consider how this learning can support and enhance ethical police practice.*

CHAPTER SUMMARY

This chapter examined how a professional standards culture that has a learning ethos can help inform ethical police strategy and practice. Such a learning culture requires an independent oversight of police misconduct – an independent agency that is empowered with its own investigatory authority. The chapter assessed how the Taylor Review provided the vehicle for a philosophical shift in disciplinary procedures, from one based on punishment and sanction to one of learning and responsible behaviour; a change from enforcing a 'disciplinary code' towards a 'code of conduct'. The disciplinary process was reviewed through the departments and organisations specifically tasked with dealing with professional standards. The development of the IPCC, tasked with independently investigating police complaints, has engendered and supported a learning philosophy in relation to disciplinary procedures, allowing misconduct to be considered within a principled approach to changing the behaviour of the individual. In addition, the IPCC, following concerns expressed in the Scarman and Macpherson Reports about the lack of public confidence in the police investigating their own complaints, was to restore trust and legitimacy in the police.

REFERENCES

Boggan, S (1992) Police Draw Up a Code of Ethics. *The Independent*, 15 August.

Covey, SR (1989) *The Seven Habits of Highly Effective People*. London: Simon and Schuster.

Goleman, D (1996) *Emotional Intelligence: Why it can matter more than IQ*. London: Bloomsbury Publishing.

HMIC (Her Majesty's Inspectorate of Constabulary) (1999) *Police Integrity: Securing and maintaining public confidence*. London: Home Office.

HMIC (Her Majesty's Inspectorate of Constabulary) (2006) *Inspection of Suffolk Police Professional Standards.* London: Home Office.

Hughes, J (2011) Theory of Professional Standards and Ethical Policing, in MacVean, A, Spindler, P and Solf, C (eds) *The Handbook of Professional Standards: Confidence, trust and integrity.* Goole: New Police Bookshop.

Jackson, L (2011) Policing the Police: Investigating professional standards, in MacVean, A, Spindler, P and Solf, C (eds) *The Handbook of Professional Standards: Confidence, trust and integrity.* Goole: New Police Bookshop.

Macpherson, Sir William (1999) *Report of the Stephen Lawrence Inquiry.* London: HMSO.

Miller, J (2003) *Police Corruption in England and Wales: An assessment of current evidence.* Online Report 11/03. London: The Home Office.

Neyroud, P and Beckley, A (2001) *Policing, Ethics and Human Rights.* Cullompton: Willan.

Punch (2010) *Shoot to Kill: Police, firearms and fatal force.* Bristol: Policy Press.

Scarman, Lord (1981) *A Report into the Brixton Disturbances of 11/12 April 1981.* London: Home Office.

Taylor, W (2005) *The Review of the Police Disciplinary Arrangements Report.* London: Home Office.

Taylor, W (2011) The Taylor Review, in MacVean, A, Spindler, P and Solf, C (eds) *The Handbook of Professional Standards: Confidence, trust and integrity.* Goole: New Police Bookshop.

USEFUL WEBSITES

www.acpo.police.uk – Association of Chief Police Officers

www.homeoffice.gov.uk – Home Office

www.ipcc.gov.uk – Independent Police Complaints Commission

www.justice.gov.uk – Ministry of Justice

www.skillsforjustice-nosfinder.com – Skills for Justice, National Occupational Standards

11 The new police professionalism: evidence, legitimacy and democracy

CHAPTER OBJECTIVES

By the end of this chapter you should be able to:

- appreciate the implications of the scientific evidence on 'what works?' for the strategies and tactics of policing and the ethical implications of this;
- understand the concept of legitimacy and the research evidence on its implications for policing and police ethics;
- appreciate the implications of democratic accountability and democratic principles for policing;
- consider the future implications for policing of the 'new professionalism'.

LINKS TO STANDARDS

This chapter provides opportunities for links with the following Skills for Justice, National Occupational Standards (NOS) for Policing and Law Enforcement 2008.

AE1.1 Maintain and develop your own knowledge, skills and competence.
CA1 Use law enforcement actions in a fair and justified way.

With the introduction of the Qualification and Credit Framework (QCF), it is likely that the term 'National Occupational Standards' will change. At the time of writing it is not clear what the new title will be, although it is known that some organisations will use the term 'QCF assessment units'.

Links to current NOS are provided at the start of each chapter; however, it should be noted that these are currently subject to review and it is recommended that you visit the Skills for Justice website to check the currency of all the NOS provided: www.skillsforjustice-nosfinder.com.

Introduction

Policing is changing rapidly and in this final chapter we want to set out three key areas of change and the reasons why they have significant implications for future ethics in policing. The three areas are:

- evidence-based policing and innovation in policing;

- police legitimacy;

- democracy and policing.

Stone and Travis (2011) have argued that these three areas are critical to the development of a 'new police professionalism', which can be contrasted with an older professionalism. The latter was developed in the 1960s and was a response to the injection of technology into policing brought about by the telephone, 999 (or in the USA, 911) emergency systems, the motor car and the radio. Kelling and Moore (1998) showed how that version of professional policing became based around response to emergencies, random patrol of public space and the investigation of volume crime. By the early 1980s, the approach had been shown to be ineffective: there was little evidence that responding to emergencies faster produced less crime or more detections; random patrol was shown to have little impact on crime (Kelling et al., 1974); the police role in investigating crime was shown to be subordinate to the contribution of witnesses and victims (Greenwood et al., 1977). In short, police appeared to be more symbolic than effective in tackling crime.

Policing entered a 'nothing works' era that prompted the development of the community policing movement, which we referred to in Chapter 5. The 'nothing works' era was neatly summed up by Professor David Bayley:

> *The police do not prevent crime. This is one of the best kept secrets of modern life. The Experts know it, the police know it, but the public does not know it. Yet the police pretend that they are society's best defence against crime . . . . This is a myth.*

(1994, p3)

Yet, only ten years later, the National Research Council in the USA pronounced that:

> *There is strong evidence supporting the effectiveness of focused and specific policing strategies. The more that strategies are tailored to the problems they seek to address, the more effective police will be in controlling crime and disorder.*

(NRC, 1994, p328)

Since then, as we will see, the quantity and quality of evidence supporting the effectiveness of some police strategies has changed enormously, presenting police leaders with a new challenge about how to adopt evidence-based approaches that demonstrably work but present some different ethical and managerial issues to the old professionalism (Weisburd and Neyroud, 2011).

Alongside this, a growing body of research has identified that it is not just what the police do but also the way that they do it that matters to the citizen (Tyler, 2003). This research, concerned with the concept of 'legitimacy', is challenging the way that police go about basic law enforcement tasks, such as stop and search, arrest and charge, and indicating that perceptions of fairness by citizens and offenders may be at least as important as the enforcement activity in both securing support for the police and encouraging law keeping in society. Fairness, or perceived fairness, is clearly a key component of ethical policing.

Finally, there has been an increasing emphasis on the relationship between democracy and policing. Over the last 30 years, police, on both sides of the Atlantic, have been made subject to increasing levels of oversight – independent investigation of complaints and misconduct, external scrutiny of performance and, in the USA, Consent Decrees that allow Federal courts to impose tight conditions on how local police departments are run or, in the UK, powers for Ministers to intervene in 'failing' police forces. There has also been a trend for politicians to take more detailed control of the policy and priorities of policing. The most obvious manifestation of this in the UK is the creation of the role of directly elected 'Police and Crime Commissioners' (PCCs) in the Police and Social Responsibility Act 2011. How the priorities for policing are set, the relationship between politics and policing and the ways in which police forces balance the needs of different communities are central to ethics. As Neyroud and Beckley observed:

> Good policing in the twenty-first century requires more than 'good performance'. It needs a renewal of the contract between the police officer and the citizen, which in turn requires greater openness and scrutiny, continuously improving professional standards and a new commitment to ethics at the core of policing.
>
> (2001, p220)

REFLECTIVE TASK

Consider the role of a Police and Crime Commissioner (PCC) directly elected to be responsible for a local police force.

- *Think how PCCs can support and enhance ethical approaches to policing and how their approach might erode it.*

- *What are the implications for a Chief Constable – appointed by and in office 'at the will' of the PCC – if he or she considered that what the PCC was asking to be done potentially conflicted with ethical standards in policing?*

- *Examine the provisions of Part 1 of the Police Reform and Social Responsibility Act 2011 at www.legislation.gov.uk/ukpga/2011/13/contents/enacted and think how the arrangements for PCC, Chief Constable and Policing and Crime Panel could be developed to strengthen ethical standards in policing.*

Evidence-based policing

The term 'evidence-based policing' (EBP) is a relatively recent one and has been defined by Sherman:

> Evidence-based policing is the use of the best available research on the outcomes of police work to implement guidelines and evaluate agencies, units and officers. Put more simply, evidence-based policing uses research to guide practice and evaluate practitioners. It uses the best evidence to shape the best practice. It is a systematic effort to parse out and codify unsystematic 'experience' as the basis for police work, refining it by ongoing systematic testing of hypotheses.
>
> (1998, p1)

The key term is 'systematic', because the first key distinction of EBP is a commitment to high standards of research evidence to underpin key aspects of practice. Second, it is argued that EBP has significant advantages over the way that knowledge has traditionally been developed in policing. This has essentially been an experience-based or clinical model – learning comes from practice and practice develops learning. David Weisburd (2011) has argued that the evidence-based approach has significant benefits over the clinical approach.

Clinical versus evidence-based model

Clinical model

- Innovation is identified, developed and diffused primarily on the basis of the experiences and opinions of practitioners.
- Clinical experience is *the* basis for decision making, not just one part of the process.

Evidence-based model

- Programmes and practices based on science (basic research) *and* clinical experience.
- Implemented first under pilot experimental conditions.
- Not widely diffused until there is evidence of effectiveness, testing for 'cures that harm'.

(Adapted from Weisburd, 2011)

Weisburd suggests that EBP reduces the risks of failure and harm from policing strategies by testing them in a controlled way before they are implemented more widely. Just as in medical practice, where doctors are required to do 'no harm' to their patients, EBP encourages police practitioners to take care to understand all the impacts of their policies, focus their efforts on the most effective aspects and mitigate the adverse consequences. Weisburd and Neyroud (2011) have argued that this is an essential basis for a genuinely professional police service.

The developing body of knowledge does, however, present dilemmas of its own. The studies of police strategies have demonstrated that police can be most effective by concentrating their efforts (Durlauf and Nagin, 2011). Many of the most important of these studies have been based on 'randomised control trials', or experiments that use techniques similar to the way that drugs or medical treatments are tested. Central to the design is the need to isolate the causal link between a proposed police strategy and its effect, and a range of potentially biasing factors such as time of day, season, location, characteristics of the population, so that it is as clear as possible that the strategy is causing any changes observed rather than other factors.

CASE STUDY

The Jacksonville patrol experiment

Focusing police efforts on 'hot spots' has gained acceptance among researchers and practitioners. However, researchers wanted to test how different strategies would per-form when compared to each other in similar areas. In order to do this, the researchers randomly assigned 83 hot spot locations, where violent crime was centred, in Jacksonville, Florida, to receive either a problem-oriented policing (POP) strategy, directed-saturation patrol, or a control condition of 'normal' policing for 90 days.

They then examined crime in these areas during the intervention period and a 90-day post-intervention period. They discovered that the use of POP was associated with a 33 per cent reduction in 'street violence' during the 90 days following the intervention and produced a significantly better outcome than either saturation patrol or 'normal policing'.

(From Taylor et al., 2010)

Such studies emphasise that there are no 'magic bullets' in policing, but there are strate-gies and tactics that work significantly better than others, for example the following.

- **Place-based strategies**:

    crime is concentrated at very small geographic units of analysis, such as street segments or small groups of street blocks. Such crime hotspots offer stable targets for interventions . . . evaluation research provides solid evidence for the effectiveness of hot spots policing.

    (Braga and Weisburd, 2010, p245)

    The research strongly suggests that police should focus their patrol and problem-solving efforts on a small number of locations. Implicitly, this means making a choice to focus a lot less effort and fewer resources on other places.

- **Offender-based strategies**: Berk et al. (2009) have demonstrated that a small group of offenders is disproportionately likely to commit the most serious crimes, whereas the vast majority of offenders present a low risk of harm. Berk at al. (2009) and Sherman and Neyroud (2011) suggest that police should focus their prosecution and investi-gative energies on the high-harm and highly persistent offenders and adopt less formal, preventive strategies with most offenders. The choices proposed are, as with the place-based approaches above, argued from a standpoint that accords greater value to effectiveness of outcome for society rather than equity of treatment for the individual citizen or offender.

- **Victim-based strategies**: Bridgeman and Hobbs, 1997) showed that people who had been victims of crime were more vulnerable to being revictimised and that some victims have a risk of multiple victimisation. They demonstrated that police strategies that focused on highly vulnerable victims could be effective at reducing crime.

Weisburd and Neyroud (2011) and Neyroud (2011) have argued, as a result, for a new approach to science in policing that would see the education of police officers and the development of police policies and practice linked to a more scientific education and a more scientific method of assessment and evaluation. Such an approach would also have benefits in encouraging the type of structured, balanced decision making that we have presented in earlier chapters of this book.

REFLECTIVE TASK

Read the publication, Policing Science: Toward a new paradigm, *by Weisburd and Neyroud at www.hks.harvard.edu/programs/criminaljustice/research-publications/executive-sessions/ policing and consider how the proposals would change police education and practice.*

- *Think about a policing strategy and consider how it might be developed, proposed and adopted in the two models – experience-based or evidence-based.*

- *Think about the implications for police decision making and ethics.*

Legitimacy

As we have suggested above, it is not just what the police do, but also the way that they carry out their duties, and perceptions of the fairness of the procedures that they use, that matters and that contributes to the legitimacy of the police. The importance of 'procedural fairness' in building support for police actions and encouraging law-keeping and compliance in those they deal with has been the subject of a series of important recent studies. Tyler (2003) has described 'procedural fairness' as consisting of two elements: the quality of decision making and the quality of interpersonal treatment. Key aspects of the first were seen to be the objectivity of decisions, the perceived competence of the police officer and the transparency of the decision to the recipient, including whether they had an opportunity to put their case and felt that this had been listened to. The quality of interpersonal treatment had a strong relationship with the politeness, dignity and respect accorded to them as human beings.

Two studies demonstrate well the potential operational importance of the approach. In the first, Paternoster et al. (1997) examined the data from the earlier Milwaukee Domestic Violence experiment, which had tested the relative effectiveness of different enforcement tactics in reducing the incidence of domestic violence. They concluded, from interviews with the men arrested, that their perceptions of the fairness and treatment that they had received significantly influenced their subsequent likelihood of obeying the law or reoffending.

In the second study, Mazerolle et al. (2011) carried out an experiment in Queensland, Australia, to test whether a standard operational power – the administration of a random breath test at the roadside – could be done in a way that emphasised procedural fairness and whether this would affect citizens' views of the police. They randomly assigned roadside testing stations to either the normal police approach – which emphasised speed and administrative efficiency – or a scripted procedure, which provided more explanation, more context (by providing data about deaths and serious injuries in the location) and greater care in courtesy and respect. The preliminary results indicated that *legitimacy policing improved (specifically and generally) levels of satisfaction with police, perceptions of police fairness and perceptions of police respect* (Mazerolle et al., 2011, p8).

However, as Tankebe (2009) has pointed out, the relationship between procedural justice and perceptions of legitimacy is not as simple as saying that, if the police 'treat you right and treat you fair', legitimacy will follow. As his study of police in Ghana illustrated, police are unlikely to be seen as legitimate, however procedurally fair they are, if they are not also seen as effective. His findings reinforce a consistent theme of this book that police need to do the right things *and* do them right. Even in the Queensland experiment, the positive impact on public perceptions of the breath test procedure did not extend to a general improvement in confidence in policing more widely.

REFLECTIVE TASK

Think about an encounter that you have had or have observed with a police officer or a public servant. How did the way you were treated or the way the member of public was treated affect your/their willingness to comply or assist the police officer or public servant?

Democracy, accountability and policing

Just as 'democracy' is a complex concept, so 'democratic policing' is far from straight-forward. David Sklansky, who has written one of the most important accounts of democratic policing, has pointed out: *The meaning of democratic policing will remain in flux – because our ideas about democracy and our ideas about the police will remain in flux* (2008, p191).

In a long-term study of democracy and policing by the Policy Studies Institute in the UK, Jones et al. (1994) stated: *There have been many interpretations of democratic ideas, and these differ in the emphasis they give to the various values inherent in them* (p43).

However, they identified six criteria that they felt could be distilled from the various democratic theories and that could be used to measure the degree to which democratic principles were being applied in policing.

- **Equity**: services should be fairly distributed between different groups and enforcement should be fair. There is a strong link between this principle and the discussion above about legitimacy.

- **Delivery of service**: because policing is a public good, it is important that it is delivered efficiently and effectively so that all citizens benefit.

- **Responsiveness**: in determining priorities, allocation of resources and policing strategies, the police should be *responsive to the views of a representative body* (p44).

- **Distribution of power**: the power to *determine policing policy should not be concentrated but should be distributed between a number of different bodies* (p44).

- **Information**: there should be detailed information about budgets, priorities and performance available to the public and representative bodies.

- **Redress**: there should be a means of redress for ill-treatment and a means of dismissing incompetent or corrupt junior and senior officers.

- **Participation**: As far as possible, citizens should be able to engage in a discussion of policing policy and delivery with senior and junior officers.

REFLECTIVE TASK

Look up the website of a police force in the UK and a police force in the USA and consider how far the principles set out by Jones et al. (1994) are being applied by the forces, as evidenced by their websites.

- *Are there any clear areas where the principles are not being applied?*

- *Do the websites show that the police forces are taking 'democratic principles' seriously – if so, how?*

- *How could they have enhanced this?*

- *Are there any major differences between the UK and USA?*

Jones et al.'s (1994) democratic principles have a clear and obvious overlap with ethical principles. However, as they set out in their study, the principles also expose how contested democratic policing can be.

- **Equity**: fairness is often, as Paternoster et al. (1997) showed, in the eye of the beholder and perceptions can be as important as 'objective' statistics. We have already discussed an example of how challenging this can be, when, in Chapter 4, we discussed the debate over the equity of stop and search statistics.

- **Delivery of service**: assessing the effectiveness and efficiency of the police service has been a controversial area in the UK in the years since 1994, when National Objectives were introduced and national performance targets imposed. Neyroud (2006) outlined the problems with nationally set interpretations of the meaning of these terms when seen from a local public's perspective. Jones et al. suggest that, even in 1994, the question of who set the terms of the definition – the Home Secretary or the Police Authority – was becoming contentious. The subsequent development of the National Police Performance Framework and detailed national targets had reached a point by 2009 when even the Labour government, which had driven that agenda hard for 12 years, concluded that the pendulum had swung too far and abandoned the targets in favour of a national 'Policing Pledge'.

- **Responsiveness**: this principle raises major questions about the nature of the 'representative body', which we will return to, but also the process through which the issues that are prioritised are determined.

- **Distribution of power**: a key problem for the police is how the priorities of minority groups can be drawn into policing priorities and how, where those priorities are in conflict with the views of the majority population, the conflict can be resolved. An obvious example of this potential tension lies in the relationship between the police and traveller communities. Many of the norms of our society are set around 'settled' communities rather than travelling communities. Both under human rights law and under ethical principles, police have a duty to treat traveller communities with dignity and respect and enforce the law fairly. However, some settled communities see travellers as a threat and want the police to use the law against them. Travellers have, traditionally, been poorly represented in formal local democratic institutions, which tend to rely on the electoral register, which, in turn, relies on settled residence. For police, this illustrates the need to have a wide awareness of the communities they are policing and a pluralist array of methods to reach out, listen and communicate. Democratic policing would not be complete without informal networks, but this can create tensions with regular, elected politicians who can see these approaches cutting across their own mandate.

- **Information**: the police service has made considerable efforts in the UK to provide detailed information about budgets, staffing, performance and crime patterns. However, introducing something as apparently simple as the National Crime Map – www.police.uk – has posed problems. There are certain types of crime, such as domestic violence, that would pose privacy problems if they were represented. It is currently difficult to represent the increasing volume of crime committed on the internet and, therefore, off local geography. Moreover, in order to prevent identification of the precise locations of burglaries, crimes are coded to a nearby location. As a result, the map, good though it is, does not provide an accurate picture of where crimes take place. The reality is that the conflicting interests and rights of individual victims and the wider public mean that even a national crime map is a compromise that seeks to do its best to represent the crime problems in each community.

- **Redress**: each and every system of redress also has to take into account the rights of the officers complained against or accused of misconduct or incompetence to seek their own rights of redress through the provision of legal representation, appeal processes and judicial review. As Jones et al. (1994) suggest, the system was and remains problematic, because it will always have tensions between the conflicting rights of the public and police officers.

- **Participation**: As Jones et al. (1994) outline, the extent to which the public participate in policing priority setting and in day-to-day discussion with the police has been one of the most problematic of the principles. In response to the Brixton riots in 1981, Lord Scarman (1981) recommended the establishment of a formal consultation process between the police and the community. The subsequent establishment of Section 106 committees (named after the original section of the Police and Criminal Evidence Act 1984) provided a mechanism that was *almost without exception unrepresentative and marginal to the policy-making process* (Jones et al., 1994, p307). The authors concluded that it was unrealistic to expect local consultation to be anything more than a minor influence on real priority setting and a marginal influence on policing.

The Police Study Institute (PSI) study revealed the challenges of democratic policing while also reaffirming its importance to effective policing. The literature on legitimacy, which we have already discussed, would also seem to suggest that a perception of an effective connection between policing and democratic principles may be important in establishing public support and compliance. However, as the analysis has set out, it is not an easy connection to make.

More recently, in both the USA and UK, there has been an increasing focus on one of the principles – responsiveness – and particularly on the strengthening of that principle by more direct representative democratic involvement in the control of police priorities, budgets and police chiefs. This was the argument advanced by Policy Exchange, a UK think tank, in a paper entitled 'Going Local', which proposed the idea of directly elected local commissioners (Policy Exchange, 2003). Their arguments were that the drift of control over priorities to the Home Office and the independence of Chief Officers to set policing policy needed to be replaced by a more visible, more transparent and, above all, democratically elected individual at the local level. They placed local democratic election above all the other principles as a means of ensuring democratic policing.

The Policy Exchange approach was developed into policy by the Conservatives in opposition, before being embedded in the Police and Social Responsibility Act 2011. The latter replaced the Police Authority, a Board of 17 or more local councillors and appointed independents, with a single individual 'Police and Crime Commissioner' with the power to set the budget, agree policing priorities, and appoint and dismiss the Chief Constable.

The developments that have seen much greater, direct political control of policing have major implications for the police ethics of the future. It seems likely that more of the issues of substance in policing – policy, strategy and many of the tactics – are to be decided by elected politicians and implemented by the police, rather than being developed by the police who are then held to account for their impact. Instead of a model of accountability after the fact – being held to account for what has happened, which has been the dominant model in democratic policing, it seems probable that accountability will be more premonitory – there will be a requirement to demonstrate that a particular approach advocated by the police will deliver the electoral promises made before approval is given to implement it. In some cases, this discussion and approval process might even precede an election campaign that might become, like some Mayoral and District Attorney campaigns in the USA, a debate about detailed tactical options such as the use of restorative justice (which has dominated a recent DA election in San Francisco).

If the tactics are to be held up for election, then the evidence that supports them becomes even more important for a profession of policing seeking to influence improvement and outcomes of policing. Neyroud (2011) has argued that it is vital, in this context, that policing becomes a more established and regulated profession, underpinned by an ethical commitment to evidence supporting practice. The alternative, that policing is driven by one political fashion after another, neither accords with Jones et al.'s principles of policing nor would seem calculated to overcome the many ethical and operational challenges – corruption, diversity, public protest, use of force or sustaining legitimacy in policing – that we have discussed in this book.

REFLECTIVE TASK

- Look up the websites of the main political parties and major think tanks for the manifestos for Police and Crime Commissioners. Consider how the approaches set out fit with the ethical challenges posed in this book.

- For comparison, search the web for electoral material from other countries, including the USA.

Conclusions

In this concluding chapter, we have focused on three major issues for the future of policing: the way in which the science of policing is offering better informed options about what works better; the importance of legitimacy and the growing understanding, through research, of its central importance to sustaining effective policing; and the nature and shifting development of democratic principles in policing.

We have sought to argue throughout this book that ethics and values are a critical golden thread running through good policing. We have shown just how difficult it is to maintain a consistent ethical approach. Ethical dilemmas in policing are rarely neat and clear-cut. We firmly believe, however, that such dilemmas are better tackled by a workforce for whom ethics are a central part of education and training, and are the everyday currency of their discussions about complex problems.

FURTHER READING

Sherman's *Evidence-based Policing* (1998), for the US Police Foundation, is a key document on the definition and development of the evidence-based approach. Weisburd and Neyroud's *Police Science: Towards a new paradigm* (2011) sets out an approach that builds on Sherman. Tyler's work is the seminal collection on legitimacy. David Sklansky's *Democracy and the Police* (2008) is a very readable and wide-ranging treatment of the developing ideas of democratic policing in the USA.

REFERENCES

Bayley, D (1994) *Police for the Future.* New York: Oxford University Press.

Berk, R, Sherman, L, Barnes, G, Ahlman, L Kurtz, E and Malvestuto, R (2009) Forecasting Murder within a Population of Probationers and Parolees: A high stakes application of statistical learning. *Journal of the Royal Statistical Society: Series A (Statistics in Society)*, 172: 191–211.

Braga, AA and Weisburd, D (2010) *Policing Problem Places: Crime hotspots and effective prevention.* New York: Oxford University Press.

Bridgeman, C and Hobbs, L (1997) *Preventing Repeat Victimisation: The police officer's guide.* London: Home Office Police Research Group.

Durlauf, SN and Nagin, DS (2011) Imprisonment and Crime: Can both be reduced? *Crime and Public Policy*, 10(1): 13–54.

Greenwood, P, Petersilia, J and Chaiken, J (1977) *The Criminal Investigation Process.* Lexington, MA: DC Heath.

Jones, T, Newburn, T and Smith, D (1994) *Democracy and Policing.* London: Policy Study Institute.

Kelling, GL and Moore, M (1998) *The Evolving Strategy of Policing.* Washington, DC: National Institute of Justice.

Kelling, GL, Pate, T, Dieckman, D and Brown, CE (1974) *The Kansas City Preventive Patrol Experiment: A technical report.* Washington, DC: Police Foundation.

Mazerolle, L, Bennett, S, Antrobus, E and Eggins, L (2011) *Key Findings of the Queensland Community Engagement Trial.* Briefing Paper from the Centre of Excellence in Policing and Security. Mt Gravatt, Queensland: CEPS.

Neyroud, P (2006) Ethics in Policing: Performance and the personalisation of accountability in British policing and criminal justice. *Legal Ethics*, 9(1): 16–35.

Neyroud, P (2011) *Review of Police Leadership and Training.* London: Home Office.

Neyroud, P and Beckley, A (2001) *Policing, Ethics and Human Rights.* Cullompton: Willan.

(NRC) National Research Council (1994) *Fairness and Effectiveness in Policing: The evidence.* Washington, DC: National Academies Press.

Paternoster, R, Brame, R, Bachman, R and Sherman, L (1997) Do Fair Procedures Matter? The effects of procedural justice on spousal assault. *Law and Society Review,* 31: 163–204.

Policy Exchange (2003) *Going Local.* London: Policy Exchange.

Scarman, Lord (1981) *A Report into the Brixton Disturbances of 11/12 April 1981.* London: Home Office.

Sherman, L (1998) *Evidence-based Policing.* Washington, DC: Police Foundation.

Sherman, L and Neyroud, P (2011) *Offender Desistance Policing.* Cambridge: Cambridge Institute of Criminology.

Sklansky, D (2008) *Democracy and the Police.* Stanford, CA: Stanford University Press.

Stone, C and Travis, J (2011) *Towards a New Professionalism in Policing.* Washington, DC: National Institute of Justice.

Tankebe, J (2009) Public Cooperation with the Police in Ghana: Does procedural fairness matter? *Criminology,* 47(4): 1265–93.

Taylor, B, Koper, C and Woods, D (2010) A Randomized Controlled Trial of Different Policing Strategies at Hot Spots of Violent Crime. *Journal of Experimental Criminology*, 7: 149–81.

Tyler, T (2003) Procedural Justice, Legitimacy and the Effective Rule of Law, in Tonry, M (ed.) *Crime and Justice: Review of research.* Chicago, IL: University of Chicago Press.

Weisburd, D (2011) *Science in Policing.* Presentation to the Evidence-based Policing Workshop, George Mason University. Online at www.cebcp.org (accessed 20 October 2011).

Weisburd, D and Neyroud, P (2011) *Police Science: Towards a new paradigm.* Washington, DC: National Institute of Justice.

USEFUL WEBSITES

http://gemini.gmu.edu/cebcp/matrix.html – Evidence-based Policing Matrix from the Center for Evidence-based Crime Policy, George Mason University

www.campbellcollaboration.org/library.php – Campbell Collaboration Library of Systematic Reviews contains reviews of crime and policing policies and tactics (enter search term 'crime' to access relevant documents)

www.hks.harvard.edu/programs/criminaljustice/research-publications/executive-sessions/policing – papers from the Harvard Executive Session on Policing and Public Safety

Index